A Passion
for Prayer

A PASSION FOR PRAYER

Experiencing Deeper Intimacy with God

TOM ELLIFF

CROSSWAY BOOKS • WHEATON, ILLINOIS
A DIVISION OF GOOD NEWS PUBLISHERS

A Passion for Prayer

Published by Crossway Books
       a division of Good News Publishers
       1300 Crescent Street
       Wheaton, Illinois 60187

Cover photo: International Stock

Cover design: Cindy Kiple

Printed in the United States of America

Bible quotations are taken from *The New King James Version*, copyright © 1982 by Thomas Nelson, Inc.

ISBN 0-89107-963-7

Dedicated to
Dr. Robert Gee Witty
who, at the age of ninety-one,
continues to be my
mentor and friend
AND
to the memory of his wife,
Kay Witty,
who until her death brought
me before God's throne
each day in prayer

Contents

FOREWORD

By Stephen Olford

No greater need exists in our churches and personal lives today than a new call to prayer. Indeed, I would venture to aver that prayerlessness is the most evident and endemic sin in our religious life. We cannot hope for a heaven-sent revival without *prevailing* prayer. God Himself declares: "If My people who are called by My name will humble themselves, and pray and seek My face, and turn from their wicked ways, then I will hear from heaven, and will forgive their sin and will heal their land" (2 Chronicles 7:14). In all the spiritual awakenings of biblical times and subsequent church history, there has never been a prayerless revival.

Praying through—persevering in prayer—that is what prayer is all about. Jesus emphasized this when He told the parable of the man who came at midnight to ask his friend for three loaves of bread (Luke 11:5-8). The householder in this situation could not get up without disturbing the whole family. But this friend was *persistent*. And where friendship could not prevail, his importunity (literally, "shamelessness") won through! The lesson is clear. We must not play at prayer. We must pray through until the answer comes. This does not mean that God is unwilling to answer prayer. On the contrary, the whole context teaches the very opposite! The need for persistence is designed to effect such a change in *us* that we conform to the character and will of the God who eagerly waits to hear our cry. Thus praying through implies *persistence* in prayer. Jesus said, "Ask . . . seek . . . knock" (Luke 11:9).

Prevailing prayer also includes *obedience* in prayer. Jesus taught that we "should always pray and not give up" (Luke 18:1), that we should be obedient in prayer. So often our praying is determined by how we *feel*! And that is all wrong. Prayer is the obedient choice of the will. Failure to obey is sin.

Praying through also involves *resistance* in prayer. James employs three aorist imperatives to ram this home: "Submit yourselves, then, to God. Resist the devil, and he will flee from you. Come near to God and He will come near to you" (James 4:7-8). Sometimes our prayers are hindered or delayed by satanic powers, and we have to resist the Devil (see Daniel 10:10-21). In C. S. Lewis's book *Screwtape Letters*, a demon sends a corrective letter to his assistant Wormwood on the need to destroy prayer. He warns, "Interfere at any price and in any fashion when people start to pray, for *real prayer is lethal to our cause.*"

Tom Elliff has proven these principles of prayer on the mission field, in the pulpit ministry, and in the leadership of a great denomination. Now he wants to share them in book form with a worldwide readership. He certainly has my blessing. My own life has been challenged afresh as I have perused these chapters. I pray; but do I pray enough? I pray; but do I have a passion for prayer?

John Wesley urged people in his day to "harness the power of persevering prayer." He wrote: "Bear up the hands that hang down, by faith and prayer. Support the tottering knees. Fast and pray. Storm the throne of grace and *persevere* therein and mercy will come down." Oh, how desperately we need divine mercy! But it will only come down when God's people unite in persevering, passionate prayer.

STEPHEN F. OLFORD
Founder and Senior Lecturer
The Stephen Olford Center for Biblical Preaching
Memphis, Tennessee

PREFACE

Why has a practice so passionately pursued by Jesus become so often ignored by those who call Him Lord? Where are the believers who have our Lord's passion for prayer? Of all the disciplines of the Christian life, it is perhaps the most neglected.

The brief years in the earthly life of our Lord were permeated with prayer. The greater the task, the greater the intensity with which He prayed. On some occasions He quietly slipped away to a place of communion with the Father. At other times the tremendous burdens of His ministry required that He send His followers away so He could gain precious moments for intercession. Our Lord prayed before the cross, on the cross, and after His resurrection. And even now a significant aspect of our eternal salvation rests upon the fact that "He always lives to make intercession" (Heb. 7:25). Little wonder that His followers begged Him, "Lord, teach us to pray" (Luke 11:1).

The results of prayer can easily be seen in the life of our Lord. The practice of prayer enabled Him to recognize those demands and ministry opportunities that were truly important. Jesus wasted no words or motions; the priorities of His life were established through prayer.

What a contrast to the believer who struggles with the nagging awareness that he is accomplishing little that is truly worthwhile. Pushed around by pressing circumstances, he feels like he is winning

some battles but losing the war. Minutes, hours, days, and years seem
to be wasted on matters that have little, if any, eternal significance.

Is there persevering prayer in *our* lives, any passion for conversation with God? The command to pray is not in question. God's Word
abounds with commands, examples, promises, and encouragements to
pray. What is missing is the obedient, heaven-bending, hell-binding
practice of prayer.

It is profitable to consider God's commands and then examine our
own experience. We are told, for instance, that we "always ought to
pray and not lose heart" (Luke 18:1). But we generally do not think
of prayer *until* we become disheartened. Many have reduced prayer to
a matter of mere etiquette. Encouraged to "pray without ceasing" (1
Thess. 5:17), we carefully ensure that our meetings never start or cease
without praying. We are careful not to eat a meal before praying. But
beyond that, do we pray?

Do you have a *praying habit*? Could you be accused of being
called "Camel-knees" as was James, our Lord's half-brother and the
pastor of the Jerusalem church, because of the calluses on his knees as
a result of endless hours of prayer?

Do you have the *praying confidence* of George Müller who
sought God alone for the needs of thousands of orphans? He refused
to ask any man for anything. Yet his carefully kept diary chronicles
God's daily, sometimes hourly, never-failing provisions.

Can you claim the *praying consistency* of Hudson Taylor, founder
of the great China Inland Mission? Those who traveled with him
recorded that no matter how grueling the day, you would hear the rus-
tle behind his curtain and see the flickering candle as he rose a few
hours past midnight to have his time with God.

Have you experienced the *praying effectiveness* of "Praying"
John Hyde, missionary to India? Though his ministry spanned only a
few years, thousands were born into the kingdom in answer to the
prayers of this man who trusted God for one, then two, then three, and
before his death, four souls each day.

Do you know something of the *praying passion* of David
Brainerd? Sickly, weak, destined to live only a few years, he determined
to share the light of the Gospel with the Indians on the eastern

seaboard of America. Faithful in witness and intercession, sometimes praying for hours in knee-deep snow, he was privileged to see one of the greatest movings of God in the history of the North American continent.

Whether you are currently making a habit of prayer or are neglecting this essential spiritual discipline, you can today and tomorrow and the next day be faithful to your Savior in your prayer life. What a glorious calling is yours—to pray, to keep praying, and to pray passionately—to persevere in communication with God until you have the assurance that God is answering and is working in the situation about which you have prayed.

> *Seeing then that we have a great High Priest who has passed through the heavens, Jesus the Son of God, let us hold fast our confession. For we do not have a High Priest who cannot sympathize with our weaknesses, but was in all points tempted as we are, yet without sin.* Let us therefore come boldly to the throne of grace, that we may obtain mercy and find grace to help in time of need.
>
> —HEBREWS 4:14-16

CALLED
TO PRAY

"God has given

us prayer,

not primarily

as a method

for getting things or

changing circumstances,

but as a means

of cooperating

with Him."

I

A PERSONAL
TESTIMONY

*"If My people who are called by My name will
humble themselves, and pray and seek My face, and
turn from their wicked ways, then I will hear
from heaven, and will forgive their sin
and will heal their land."*

2 CHRONICLES 7:14

SEVERAL YEARS AGO I BEGAN to study the lives of great people of
prayer. I could not escape the fact that God used men and women who
were dedicated to the practice of prayer to change the course of history. The more I read, the more convicted I became of my own prayerlessness. I had seen a certain measure of success in the pastorate and
was considered by some to have arrived at a most enviable position.
But now I found myself, without benefit of either human criticism or
encouragement, under the searching eye of God. Alone before Him, I
could not defend my utter lack of prayer.

It was not that I did not *appear* to be a man of prayer. A few
well-chosen words were available for any occasion. I preached about
prayer, conducted prayer meetings, and always responded in the
affirmative to those who asked, "Pastor, will you pray for me?" "I'll
be praying for you" were the last words of every pastoral visit. Each
letter closed with the assurance, "You can count on our continued

prayers." But in reality, my personal prayer altar was in ruins. Except for spasmodic periods of renewed effort, I just did not pray.

Now God had found me out. Or rather, God was allowing me to find out about myself. My prayer famine had not disturbed me in times past. But now I felt as if my case had come before the court of heaven. The evidence was in; I was guilty of disobedience by gross negligence.

Unable to rest, I settled on somewhat of a trial run. Looking back now, in the light of God's promises, it all seems rather foolish. But it was serious business then—and God took me seriously. I determined to spend the morning hours in my study in uninterrupted prayer. To some people that may not sound like much. But to a pastor who considered the ministry as sort of a public relations position, it was difficult. Think of all the coffee breaks, jokes, telephone calls, and fellowship I would miss, not to mention the seemingly endless list of administration responsibilities!

When the office door closed behind me Monday morning, I took my Bible, fell to my knees, and told the Lord an out-and-out lie. "Lord, You know I have desired to have time alone with You in prayer." In less time than it takes to tell, the Lord reminded me that for the most part we do what we want to do. I was forced to agree that I had not had time for prayer because I had not taken the time to pray.

I confess that I frequently glanced at my watch during those first few minutes of prayer. Each minute seemed to take forever. I discovered that I was not really accustomed to communion with God. I felt uncomfortable as I framed the words, wondering how they would sound to others. Praying for all the usual people, events, and needs did not dispel the uneasiness I felt.

It was obvious that God wanted to do business on a deeper level— God wanted to deal with my personal rebellion. A great barrier of unconfessed sin had to crumble under the forgiveness of God during the next few hours. Cleansed by the work of Jesus, according to 1 John 1:9, I began to see more clearly the issues confronting the members of my congregation. It was then that I began to pray in earnest for them.

At noon I opened the door of my study only to discover a stranger waiting to visit for "just a moment." "Pastor," he said, "you don't know me. I was just driving by the church, and something told me to come in here and ask you how I could get saved." In a matter of minutes he was born into God's family. He then rushed to meet his wife and led her to Christ. At noon on the next two days similar experiences awaited me when I opened the door of my study after a morning of prayer. In addition, it seemed that God protected that time from any interruptions (unexpected phone calls, forgotten meetings, etc.). Church members clearly appreciated their pastor's desire to be available to God.

God continued to deal with me graciously as I spent more time with Him. During the next two weeks, over 100 individuals walked the aisle of our church during invitation times. More than half of them desired to profess Christ as Lord and Savior. In the events of those weeks God convinced me that He intends prayer to be a vital tool in the Christian's walk and warfare.

Twenty-five years have passed since God's Spirit brought that prayer revival to my heart. Those years have taken me across the United States and to many countries of the world, including a brief time as a missionary in Africa. Today I am more convinced than ever that prayer is both the believer's most powerful and most unused weapon.

I have learned that the secret is *praying a matter through* to its proper conclusion—to persevere in intercession until we receive God's resolution of a needy situation. It is my intent in this book to share some of the basic principles of prayer and, more specifically, to show how these principles relate to persevering in prayer and to healthy, victorious Christian living.

I have also discovered that God is keenly interested in the personal life of the one who is praying. This is especially true when one assumes the position of an intercessor. God has given us prayer, not primarily as a method for getting things or changing circumstances, but as a means of cooperating with Him in His great plan for the redemption of the lost and other great spiritual exploits.

A clear example of intercession is recorded in Genesis 18, where we read about the Lord and two other messengers meeting with Abraham and Sarah to affirm God's promise of a son through whom all the nations of the world would be blessed. Afterwards, as the visitors set their faces toward Sodom, the Lord said, "Shall I hide from Abraham what I am doing? . . . For I have known him, in order that he may command his children and his household after him, that they keep the way of the LORD, to do righteousness and justice" (vv. 17-19). The Lord then explained His purpose for going to Sodom and Gomorrah by noting that their "sin is very grave" (v. 20).

Abraham became distressed because his nephew, Lot, lived in Sodom. The Scripture records that "the men turned away from there and went toward Sodom, but Abraham still stood before the LORD" (v. 22). It was then that Abraham began to intercede for the welfare of Lot and his family. Persistent in prayer, he finally secured this promise from the Lord: "I will not destroy it [Sodom] for the sake of ten [righteous people]" (v. 32). It was then that "the LORD went his way . . . and Abraham returned to his place" (v. 33). Abraham had "prayed through" for Lot; he had interceded effectively, and as a result Lot did not die along with the others in Sodom. Godly prayer makes a difference!

From these verses we see that intercession requires aggressive cooperation with God along the lines of His revealed will. Additionally, we see that intercession involves imploring God on behalf of a specific person or persons.

Other Bible portions also touch on this important topic, some of which are neglected by many believers. It is unfortunate, for example, that many Christians consider the passages of Scripture describing the tabernacle in the wilderness a drudgery to read. Actually, the tabernacle can be seen to represent three basic areas of our lives. The outer courtyard surrounded by a high curtain represents the externally visible part of our being—the body. The holy place, a place of daily activity within the confines of the tent-like structure, represents the soul. The holy of holies represents the spirit, or our capacity for communion with the Lord. Similarly, the altar of incense represents Christ's ministry of intercession for us and the qualities in His life that we are to emulate. These qualities are specifically outlined in Exodus 30:1-10. Three of them appear to be of particular significance regarding the practice of prayer:

POSITION

Intercession is as much the *taking of a position* as it is the *making of a petition*. Exodus 30:6 states that the altar of incense was to be placed "before the veil that is before the ark of the Testimony, before the mercy seat that is over the Testimony, where I [God] will meet with you." In other words, the altar of incense was positioned between the mercy seat and everything else in the tabernacle. It was the last component the high priest saw before entering the holy of holies. An intercessor's position is both *before God* and *between God and the person for whom he is interceding.*

As we saw earlier, "Abraham still stood before the LORD." Abraham was both before the Lord and between the Lord and Sodom where Lot was living in sin. To position yourself before someone is to say, "There is a matter that you and I must settle before I can continue on." That is what Abraham was saying, and that is what we will say if we engage in intercession.

PERSEVERANCE

Furthermore, incense was to be burned on the altar both morning and evening, "a perpetual incense before the LORD throughout your generations" (Exod. 30:7-8). Here is where great spiritual battles are often won or lost. At issue is the willingness to "pray without ceasing" (1 Thess. 5:17) until God reveals His will about the issue of concern.

Persevering prayer is the experience of few Christians. They are willing, when asked, to pray for certain individuals. Perhaps they even enter that person's name on a daily prayer list. But most believers know little about bowing before God and remaining there *until* He reveals His will.

Individuals wholeheartedly engaged in the ministry of intercession have a hard time thinking of anything else. They have before them the daily demands of their occupations, but even these are carried out with the inner man bowed before God.

Sometimes "concerned" Christians ask me to pray with them about certain people. But on subsequent days these Christians make no further mention of their concern. In contrast, others request prayer and really do appear to have assumed the position of an intercessor. Every time I see them, they report on the status of the individuals for whom they have asked prayer. Often they report with tears of joy how God is bringing blessing to their lives by allowing them to enter into aggressive cooperation in His great work.

Luke 11:5-8 records Jesus' parable emphasizing the importance of shameless persistence in prayer:

> *"Which of you shall have a friend, and go to him at midnight and say to him, 'Friend, lend me three loaves: For a friend of mine has come to me on his journey, and I have nothing to set before him'; and he will answer from within and say, 'Do not trouble me; the door is now shut, and my children are with me in bed; I cannot rise and give to you.' I say to you, though he will not rise and give to him because he is his friend, yet because of his persistence he will rise and give him as many as he needs."*

It was not the size of the need, the cause of the need, or the credentials of the one in need that finally secured the answer. It was the man's "persistence." The Lord concluded the parable with this statement: "Ask [literally, keep on asking], and it will be given to you; seek [literally, keep on seeking], and you will find; knock [literally, keep on knocking], and it will be opened to you" (v. 9). It is little wonder that the enemy seeks so actively to destroy the Christian's determination to *persevere* in prayer.

PURITY

There was a strict formula for the type of incense to be burned on the altar in the tabernacle. God admonished the priests, "You shall not offer *strange* incense on it, or a burnt offering, or a grain offering; nor shall you pour a drink offering on it" (Exod. 30:9). Only *pure* incense was to be offered.

If there is one point more than any other at which we are defeated in prayer, it is at the point of personal purity. God hates sin. It is an abomination to Him; it cost Him His Son. We often fail to deal with sin in biblical terms, calling it instead a bad habit, shortcoming, or character flaw. Some people hold to the notion that sin can be held at bay in an otherwise righteous life. This is like telling your friends you are in perfect health though you are aware of a malignancy growing in your body. Your sin, no matter how secret, affects your ability and the ability of your church to pray. Proverbs 15:8 reminds us that "the sacrifice of the wicked is an abomination to the LORD." In other words, even our best efforts to please God fail as long as we harbor any wickedness or impurity in our heart.

Christians seem especially susceptible to sins of presumption (see Psalm 19:13), sins that presume on God's love and forgiveness. Consider, for instance, a man seated in a worship service who can't wait for the service to end so he can indulge in his favorite sinful habit. By his life he is saying in essence, "God, You are loving and forgiving. Turn Your head while I sin. But be quick to forgive when I ask." We must weed out all such wrong thinking and improper living.

Our prayers are answered only when we pray "in Jesus' name," that is, on the basis of what He has accomplished and who He is. How many times we have knelt to pray, only to be confronted by the master of accusation, Satan himself. "You don't really think this is going to do any good, do you? Your life is no example of victory. How can *you* presume to be in touch with God?" Defeated by such words, and failing to see the effectiveness of the grace of God in our own lives, we question His power in the lives of others. Satan uses our sin to keep us from praying for others.

Intercession involves aggressive cooperation with the revealed will of Him who can have no fellowship with sin. The psalmist writes: "Who may ascend into the hill of the LORD? Or who may stand in His holy place? He who has clean hands and a pure heart" (Ps. 24:3-4). "Behold, the LORD's hand is not shortened, that it cannot save; nor His ear heavy, that it cannot hear. But your iniquities have separated you from your God; and your sins have hidden His face from you, so that He will not hear" (Isa. 59:1-2). The heart's cry of every Christian who yearns to labor in the fields of intercession should be, "Create in me a clean heart, O God, and renew a steadfast spirit within me" (Ps. 51:10).

The person who participates in Olympic competition spends years preparing his body and mind for a specific event of only temporal importance. In light of the billions of people who are alienated from God or who have been saved but are struggling or stumbling, how can we afford *not* to spend time preparing our hearts and lives for the eternally significant work of intercession?

We should each look closely at God's pattern for the intercessor. Ask Him for enough grace to assume the position, pray with perseverance, and seek the purity that is crucial for effective intercession. Ask Him to enable you to persevere in prayer!

QUESTIONS FOR REFLECTION AND PRAYER

1. Do you have a faithful practice of prayer, or merely an appearance of being a man or woman of prayer? Why? Are you content with this, or do you desire substantial change? Offer praise or prayer to God about this right now.

2. What are you willing to sacrifice in order to become a person of great prayer? What steps can you take to make this a reality in your life? What results do you hope will come from this? Talk to God in detail about this right now.

3. Making a petition—taking a position—persevering in intercession for others—praying with a pure heart—in which of these areas do you struggle most? Why? With what effects? In which areas do you experience the most victory? With what results? Discuss this with God right now.

2

RECOVERING OUR
INTIMACY WITH GOD

Today, if you will hear His voice:
"Do not harden your hearts."

PSALM 95:7-8

LOSING AN INTIMATE SENSE of God's presence is a sobering experience. Such a state may come as a result of flagrant rebellion, or it may
be the culmination of many seemingly minor choices to resist God's
clear leadership. Whatever the cause, it is disturbing to sense in ourselves or others a growing hardness of heart and an accompanying
helplessness to recover from it.

Many believers are under the misconception that they can return
to intimacy with the Lord whenever they want. They believe restored
fellowship is solely a matter of their personal discretion, available at
the drop of a hat. But in moments of deep searching and quiet desperation they admit that even the willingness to will themselves back
to God is missing. They come to the startling revelation that we must
come to Him on His terms and at His time or we will not come at all.

The underlying plea of Psalm 95 is that we guard against the hardening of our hearts. To illustrate the nature of such a dangerous spiritual
state, the psalmist refers to a critical moment in Israel's history. While
the people were camped at Kadesh Barnea, God instructed Moses to
send spies into neighboring Canaan, the Promised Land (Num. 13).
Their report was meant to encourage the recently delivered Israelites.

But the spies brought *discouragement* instead. With Joshua and Caleb as notable exceptions, the spies acknowledged the land's abundance but focused primarily on the giants, the sons of Anak, before whom the Israelites were like grasshoppers. Angry and terrified, the Jewish nation rejected the pleas of Moses, Joshua, and Caleb to do what God had told them to do. Their refusal to follow God brought His wrath, and the disobedient generation was sentenced to wander and ultimately die in the wilderness they had preferred over Canaan.

After a night of reflection on God's judgment, the children of Israel repented and returned to Moses, expressing a willingness to go in and conquer Canaan. "It is too late," Moses warned them. But they refused to hear him and mounted a battle that cost the lives of many. The lesson was clear: God had opened a window of opportunity that they neglected, and their refusal to immediately obey was costly. Their hardened hearts had cost them and their families dearly. God would give Canaan to another generation of faith.

God calls believers to prayer. He is calling you! He is calling me! Through prayer we are, figuratively speaking, to occupy the land and enjoy the fruit of His promises—to accomplish whatever He intends and to step out by faith in Him. He is today the same God as Israel's God, and the need for immediate obedience is unchanged. Also unchanged are the consequences when we fail to obey. With every delay, opportunities are lost.

A CALLING MASTER

The call to prayer tests our comprehension of God. If we know Him, if we rightly understand the truth about who He is and what He desires of us, prayer is a welcome invitation. Can we ignore His call? Can we substitute our own plans for God's? Yes, but not without disastrous consequences. Is there anything God will accept in place of simple obedience to Him? No. Nothing at all.

Notice *the profound significance of this call*. The urgency of our response to any voice is directly related to the personal significance of the one who is calling. Just watch a cluster of mothers visiting with one another around a picnic bench in a crowded park. Amid the clamor of playing children they sit calmly until one of them hears the voice of *her* child. That is a voice she knows, a call she will not disregard.

The One who is calling you to prayer is your Savior (Ps. 95:1), your Sovereign (v. 7), your Sustainer (v. 4), your Source and Maker (vv. 5-6), and your Shepherd (v. 7). He has charged Himself with the responsibility for your welfare. *He* is the One who calls you. Will you ignore His voice?

I remember a congressional hearing in which a lieutenant colonel in the Marines was asked how he would respond to any request the President of his country might make. He noted that his President was also his Commander-in-chief and that no request, however ridiculous it might seem, would be denied. He knew that in human terms the President holds ultimate authority for American citizens and soldiers. Here the psalmist is not referring to an earthly commander-in-chief but to our Sovereign Lord, the God to whom we must all answer and who invites all His children to approach Him in prayer.

Notice also *the personal subject of this call.* Frequently when I speak on university campuses, I am asked how we can recognize the call of God. My response is simple. Knowing is inherent in the call. You know God is speaking *to you.* God is a powerful communicator, and He speaks with distinction.

When I was a child my mother would come to the front door of our house and call, "Tommy! Come in and wash your hands! It's time for supper!" Some things were obvious in that situation. This was *my* mother. She was calling *me.* I knew *what* she wanted. And I knew that as far as my mother was concerned, obedience was either *immediate* or it was not obedience.

"Today, if *you will* hear His voice," pleads the psalmist. When God speaks, you know He is *speaking to you.* And as far as He is concerned, obedience is either immediate or it is not obedience at all.

Finally, note *the particular sound of this call.* People often hide their disobedience behind the skirts of feigned ignorance. "I didn't know what the Lord wanted me to do." Our faith must come to the level of maturity that accepts that God holds us accountable for all our decisions. Sufficient knowledge of His will is always available so that we can respond appropriately.

The "voice" to which the psalmist refers is not some muffled, indistinguishable sound. It is the clarion call of God. As a friend of mine once said, "There are times when I *think* God is speaking to me. But when God really speaks to me, I *know* it is God who is speaking!" Again, God is a clear communicator.

Our Master is calling us to pray and to persevere in prayer. He may be addressing other issues in our lives as well. Perhaps the issue is our devotional life—the necessity of spending time regularly in His presence. Maybe it has to do with some breach of personal or moral integrity. It could be that He is addressing the matter of our steward-ship. Or He might be asking us to make adjustments in our relation-ships with others in our homes, in our neighborhoods, at church, or at work. Whatever the particular situation, the Master is calling us. Will we harden our hearts, or will we obey Him?

A CONTRARY MIND-SET

Why does the psalmist plead with us, "Do not harden your hearts"? Why does the writer of Hebrews focus such attention on that kind of heart (chapters 3—4)? Is it possible that the consequences of a hard-ened heart are more costly than we imagine? Why is God so concerned about this type of spiritual condition? There are three significant reasons.

Hardening your heart requires a conscious effort. It is something you do to yourself. "Do not harden *your* hearts," writes the psalmist. We must make a deliberate choice to respond to God rather than to resist His leadership and suffer serious consequences.

Occasionally I meet people who try to excuse their own bitterness by detailing the circumstances they believe have brought it about. In reality they have brought it upon themselves; they have chosen not to respond properly. Inevitably you can find someone who has walked through circumstances that are similar or worse and yet came out with a sensitive heart and a gracious spirit. These people made right choices in regard to difficult situations. You cannot always control your cir-cumstances, but you *can* (and do) choose your response.

I was once approached by a man driven with an obsession to bring down a company that had terminated his employment. His choice to ignore Scripture and take vengeance into his own hands had made him a bitter, cynical, resentful man. Little did he know that his rage was even bringing on physical consequences that would ultimately cause an untimely death. Throughout our conversation he was determined to show me what "they" had done to him. Like the ten fearful spies, he was more taken with the size of the giants than with the size of his God. He refused to make room in his life for mercy or for God's grace, preferring to allow hatred to fester and conquer his heart.

Unfortunately, his story is not unusual. Many people have hardened hearts because of their ongoing refusal to submit to a sovereign Lord. They must bear personal responsibility for such hard-heartedness. It cannot be blamed on God or others since it is the result of their conscious choice.

Hardening your heart also registers a cumulative effect. The effect of wrong choices increases with each successive resistance, making further disobedience even easier. As William Mason states, "Each day we wait to obey God leaves one more day to repent of and one less day to repent in." Hard-heartedness can easily become habitual, closing our hearts more and more to God and making it harder and harder to engage in regular prayer and worship.

The Hebrew word translated "harden" in this passage refers to the process by which something is made dense or thick. It is the picture of a callus, the successive layers of skin that develop to resist irritation. Maybe some of us sense such a condition in our own hearts. Perhaps God has been speaking to us about some issue, but we have not yet responded with surrender. Perhaps we sense a loss of fellowship in our relationship with God and have lost confidence in the effectiveness of prayer (which is to say, we no longer have assurance that God cares and will answer with grace). Is it possible that our current indifference to His will is just one more link in a long chain of resistance?

Furthermore, *hardening our heart results in a continuing expression.* Each time Israel resisted God, it became even easier to say no to His leading. I once heard it said of someone, "He finds it easier to climb a tree and tell a lie than to stand on the ground and tell the truth." A greater affinity for untruth than for truth makes it easy to say no to the Spirit's promptings. Israel developed a predisposition to sin that ultimately led them to practice idolatry and even child-sacrifice! The hardening of the heart is a serious matter!

We would not think of standing on a street corner, shaking our fists toward heaven, and shouting in open defiance against God. But we have less obvious ways of being just as obstinate in resisting His way for our life and ignoring the principles of His Word. We can become like the child who hears but does not obey the voices of his parents. He assumes that if they are serious, they will continue to call, but in the meantime he keeps playing outside.

God is calling us to conquer the land through prayer. What are we doing "in the meantime"? Will be pretend to be spiritually deaf, or will we return to the practice of persevering prayer?

A CRITICAL MOMENT

There is a sense of urgency in this issue that we must not overlook. "Today," exclaims the psalmist. God is calling, and He wants our response without delay. Why is it so critical that we respond *now*?

This is *the obvious time for us to respond*. Is that not the very heart of the matter—immediate obedience? Failure to respond *now* is what constitutes hard-heartedness. Failure to respond today only makes more likely our refusal to yield to God in the future.

Israel's experience should be a lesson to us all. God gave them an opportunity to possess the land, but it had to be on His terms and in His time. We must listen to and obey God's call! Isn't it obvious that He wants each of us to be or become a person of prayer today? Can we be sure that if we make no change today, we will have a heart for it tomorrow?

I have often stood at the bedside of elderly dying men who could not bring themselves to profess faith in Christ. Sadly, I can on such occasions recall moments when the heart was softer and the call more clear, but the answer was "no." Now, as they are facing eternity, these men cannot do what they have always intended to do. Death comes, and hell waits for the hardened heart, and yet the procrastinator cannot come to Christ. What a tragedy! *Similarly, hard-hearted believers miss opportunities that can never be recovered.*

We must also respond now because this is *the opportune time for us to respond.* The simple rendering for the Hebrew word translated "today" is "in the warm hours." Even the secular world speaks about "hot" deals that must be seized now or lost forever.

Listen to Isaiah: "Seek the LORD *while* He may be found. Call upon Him *while* He is near" (Isa. 55:6). Why? There will come a time when He will not be found, a time when He will no longer be near and disposed to respond to our prayer.

On more than one occasion I have had adulterous men look at me sheepishly and try to excuse their sin by reminding me that King David, a "man after God's own heart," had similar problems. Usually, however, there is a distinct difference between these men and David. When David was confronted with his sin, he melted in repentance and confession. These men, however, try to excuse their disobedience by pointing to a biblical record of a good man's failure. God is convicting them, but in their warm hour they do not agree with Him and turn from their sin with a broken heart.

Finally, this is *the only time for us to respond.* Yesterday is past—and with it our opportunity to agree with God. Tomorrow has not arrived—and for any one of us it may never arrive. Only "today" is at our disposal. This is the moment when God wants us to break cycles of hard-hearted indifference and answer His call.

We must not assume we can wait until tomorrow and it will be just the same as if we had answered God today. Remember Israel's sad experience—one hour of rejection brought forty years in the wilderness. Your prayers are a vital part of God's plan. There are individuals and issues that stand in need of your prayer right now! Listen to God's Word! "Today . . . do not harden your hearts."

QUESTIONS FOR REFLECTION AND PRAYER

1. What is God saying to you these days about your prayer life? What is He calling you to do differently? Why? Converse with Him about it right now.

2. Is your mind-set generally one of surrender to God or of hard-heartedness? Why? With what results? Talk to God about the present condition of your heart.

3. What response do you need to make to God *today*? Are you willing to do this? Why or why not? What are the probable results of your choice? Discuss this with God right now.

4. What guarantee do you have that waiting to obey God will not result in consequences more serious than you can imagine? What is the basis of any assurance that it is to your advantage not to choose against God's plan today? Will you resist Him—or will you turn to Him? Tell God what is on your heart.

3

A QUIET TIME,
A QUIET PLACE

And Judas . . . knew the place;
for Jesus often met there with His disciples.

JOHN 18:2

IN YOUR BUSY LIFE do you have a quiet time and a quiet place where consistently, day by day, you can spend time in prayer with the Lord? Is that time and place so firmly established that, as in the case of Jesus or in the case of Daniel years earlier, a plot for your life could be built upon the common knowledge that at a specific time you can be found praying in a specific place?

Jesus made it clear that *the central issue regarding His lordship is obedience:* "But why do you call Me 'Lord, Lord,' and do not do the things which I say?" (Luke 6:46). And again, "Not everyone who says to Me, 'Lord, Lord,' shall enter the kingdom of heaven, but he who does the will of My Father in heaven" (Matt. 7:21). By both example and exhortation Christ constantly reminds us that "men always ought to pray and not lose heart" (Luke 18:1). Yet it is in the arena of prayer that we fail most often to obey the precepts of our Lord.

On the evening before His crucifixion, Jesus was with His disciples. They observed the Feast of the Passover together, and then, crossing over the brook Kidron, they entered the Garden of Gethsemane. Judas had already arranged his betrayal of Christ, and now he made his way through the streets of Jerusalem, followed by a cohort of

Roman soldiers. (It is estimated there were between 300 and 600 Roman soldiers with Judas that evening.) It is worth noting that Judas did not have to lead these soldiers on a wild goose chase through the streets of Jerusalem. Judas knew where Jesus could be found, for Jesus "*often met there with His disciples*." Judas knew Jesus would be in His place of prayer.

Consistency is found at the heart of effective prayer. Any book on the subject of prayer would be of little impact if in some way it did not encourage the reader to establish a pattern of faithfulness in prayer. Great prayer warriors are noted more for the faithful *maintenance* of their prayer life than for their *method* of praying. Consider what we will experience if we, like Jesus, will establish a quiet place in our lives where we can regularly spend quiet times with the Father.

COMMUNION

Prayer is, above all else, communion with God. Mark's gospel reveals that during His Gethsemane experience, Jesus entered into a time of honest, intimate fellowship with the Father (see 14:32-36). The very word He used, "Abba," is one of tender endearment. Unlike the more formal word *father*, its equivalent in our culture today would be *Daddy*. This kind of intimate communion with the Father can only be developed through a consistent prayer life.

Two observations are in order here. First, *it is folly to seek counsel from people who do not themselves seek counsel from God.* We tend to divide our lives into the secular and the spiritual. Secular matters include our finances or our job. Spiritual matters have to do with our relationship with the Lord. In secular matters, we normally do not consider the spiritual depth of the person from whom we seek advice. I know many Christians, for instance, who seek consultation regarding their finances from some of the most godless sources. On the other hand, they feel it is appropriate to seek counsel on spiritual matters only from people who are spiritually minded.

But God makes no such division between the secular and the spiritual. Our entire life is to be a spiritual offering to Him. Therefore, when we seek counsel, whatever the issue, we should consult people who appreciate and honor what God says in His Word and who as a habit converse with Him about the affairs of life.

My wife once asked our children's pediatrician specific questions about his personal relationship with Christ. He was surprised at her queries. He just assumed she knew he was a church member and a true believer in Christ. He failed to see any relationship between his spiritual life and his ability to be a good physician for our children. My wife told him that she did indeed know he was a church member, but since he would be counseling her regarding the welfare of our children, she wanted to know more about his relationship with the Lord. In particular, she was interested in knowing just how often he sought the Lord's wisdom regarding his patients. My wife is a wise woman of God.

Second, *it is equally important that we counsel others only after we have sought the counsel of the Lord.* Often we respond to people's questions carelessly. With little thought or prayer we tell them what we would do about the situation. But it is imperative for us to hear from God before dispensing advice to others.

After twenty years of pastoral counseling, I became discouraged at the realization that a small number of people consumed the major portion of my counseling time and seemed to make minimal progress. I finally realized how little prayer and thought I was giving to their problems. This brought about a significant change in my approach to counseling. Instead of giving immediate advice, I began to ask more questions about their situation and would then say, "Now that I have a grasp of the problems you are facing, I want to pray over this matter and seek the counsel of God through the Scriptures. When He gives me His answer, I will share with you what He has shared with me."

The results amazed me. Those whom I counseled placed a greater value on the words I shared; and when they followed the counsel given, their lives were changed for the better. The reason for the difference was obvious: I was seeking the counsel of God before giving advice to others. This approach required that I spend more time in prayer each day. But after all, isn't that a desired priority?

Quiet places where we spend quiet times will be places and times of intimate communion with God.

CONFLICT

Conflict is inescapable, but some handle it better than others. Individuals who maintain a calm disposition in the midst of difficult circumstances shine like bright stars against the dark horizon of chaos and confusion. Who are these people? They are those who find strength for their conflicts in quiet times of Bible reading and prayer. When asked the secret of a successful, long-term ministry, E. F. "Preacher" Hallock, then pastor of First Baptist Church in Norman, Oklahoma, responded, "Fight every battle on your knees."

Some people are under the misconception that conflict always indicates you are out of God's will. But that is certainly not the case. Moses would rarely have won a popularity contest. He went from one conflict to another, and yet, with few exceptions, he remained in the center of God's will as he led the children of Israel out of Egypt and on to the border of the Promised Land. During His earthly ministry Jesus frequently faced opposition that ultimately nailed Him to the cross. Obviously, He was *always* in the center of God's will.

Some believe the greatest struggle surrounding Christ's crucifixion took place not on the cross but in the Garden of Gethsemane. Luke's vivid account of the physical struggle that took place in the garden is most enlightening.

> *Coming out, He went to the Mount of Olives, as He was accustomed, and His disciples also followed Him. When He came to the place, He said to them, "Pray that you may not enter into temptation." And He was withdrawn from them about a stone's throw, and He knelt down and prayed, saying, "Father, if it is Your will, remove this cup from Me; nevertheless not My will, but Yours, be done." Then an angel appeared to Him from heaven, strengthening Him. And being in agony, He prayed more earnestly. Then His sweat became like great drops of blood falling down to the ground.*
> —LUKE 22:39-44

Physicians tell us that Jesus was experiencing hematadrosis, a physiological condition in which the capillary action of the blood changes to such an extent that clots of blood emerge through the pores of one's body. This occurs only when people are under severe stress. This was clearly a time of immense struggle for our Lord.

Jesus knew He would soon be arrested and falsely accused. His beard would be pulled from His battered and bruised face. A crown of thorns would pierce His scalp and scrape against His skull. Professional scourgers would beat Him with strips of leather embedded with pieces of metal and glass. They would literally beat Him within an inch of His life, a practice that frequently left visceral organs exposed through gaping wounds in the body. After carrying His cross to Golgotha, our Lord would be stretched out upon it, and heavy spikes would be driven through His extremities. His bones would be ripped from their joints as the cross was lifted up and suddenly dropped into a socket in the ground.

Crucifixion was the most excruciating means of execution ever devised by sinful man. If the person did not die from infection or loss of blood, he would gradually drown in the fluids of his own body. Able to inhale but not exhale, the chest cavity would gradually fill up with fluid. That explains why blood mixed with water flowed from the wound when the soldier pierced Jesus' side. Calvary was not a beautiful green hill. It was a filthy, foul-smelling place where the dogs prowled, the worms crawled, the flies swarmed, the crowd jeered, soldiers cursed, and the crucified screamed in agony.

In vivid contrast to all the confusion that surrounded the crucifixion, Jesus exhibited unusual calm and self-control. He did not fly off the handle; He did not lose His composure. Though the sins of all mankind were placed upon Him, He manifested tranquillity and love and died only when He *chose* to give up the spirit.

No believer's life is without difficulty. Trials are an essential part of the growth process. But when the conflicts of our lives are hammered out on the anvil of faith and prayer, we can rise to meet the enemy head-on with the knowledge that victory is assured. Our quiet times and quiet places can become Gethsemanes from which we emerge to resolutely fulfill the will of God.

CONFORMITY

From the moment of our conversion, God has one basic purpose for our lives during our earthly journey: He is conforming us to the image of His Son (Rom. 8:29).

> *When God wants to drill a man and skill a man and thrill a man;*
> *when God wants to mold a man to play the noblest part,*
> *and when He yearns with all His heart*
> *to create so great and bold a man that all the world shall be amazed,*
> *watch His method, watch His ways,*
> *how He ruthlessly perfects whom He royally elects.*
> *How He hammers him and hurts him and with mighty blows*
> *converts him into trial shapes of clay which only God understands*
> *and his tortured heart is crying and he lifts beseeching hands,*
> *how He bends but never breaks whom his good He undertakes.*
> *How He uses whom He chooses and with every purpose*
> *fuses him and by every act induces him to try His splendor out.*
> *God knows what He's about.*

— SOURCE UNKNOWN

Conformity to Christ can best occur during our quiet times with Him. Sadly, many of God's children allow so little time for the quiet place that God is forced to deal with them in the public arena. If we will not humble ourselves before God during a quiet hour, for instance, He will be forced to humiliate us publicly. One way or the other, we are destined to learn humility, one of the primary characteristics of our Lord Jesus Christ.

I have a friend who calls occasionally to ask if the Lord has shown me "some new thing." On one occasion I replied, "I've learned how to get all I want!" He responded in surprise, "That sounds rather crass." "I know it does," I responded, "but it's true nonetheless."

Here is the truth I shared with him: If I could just get to the place in my life where all I wanted was whatever God wanted for me, then I would have all I wanted, and He would have all of me that He wanted! This is the essence of conforming to His will.

Matthew's record of the Gethsemane experience addresses the issue of conformity:

> *He went a little farther and fell on His face, and prayed, saying, "O My Father, if it is possible, let this cup pass from Me; nevertheless, not as I will, but as You will." Then He came to the disciples and found them sleeping, and said to Peter, "What? Could you not watch with Me one hour? Watch and pray, lest you enter into temptation. The spirit indeed is willing, but the flesh is weak." Again, a second time, He went away and prayed, saying, "O My Father, if this cup cannot pass away from Me unless I drink it, Your will be done." And He came and found them asleep again, for their eyes were heavy. So He left them, went away again, and prayed the third time, saying the same words.*
>
> — MATTHEW 26:39-44

It appears there was a great wrestling match going on in the Garden of Gethsemane that night. Knowing the cross was before Him, Christ's humanity, in some sense, wrestled against the divine mission. Our Lord's statement, "The spirit indeed is willing, but the flesh is weak" is most likely a reference to the fact that his flesh, His humanity, was crying out against the coming agony of the cross, while that which was spiritual responded with, "Nevertheless, not as I will, but as You will." Only when there was total conformity to the will of God did our Lord come to His disciples and say, "Behold, the hour is at hand, and the Son of Man is being betrayed into the hands of sinners."

HOW WILL WE BE KNOWN?

Within the great panorama of the Bible, certain individuals stand out because of their exceptional influence and effectiveness. We are so taken with their public lives that we often overlook the depth of their private commitments. The longer I live, the more convinced I become that the greatest work of God takes place in the private arena—the quiet place, the quiet time. There God waits for us in order to have sweet communion, resolve anguishing conflict, and bring about a remarkable conformity to His Son, our Lord Jesus Christ.

The brilliant light of a Roman candle streaks across the sky, evoking the pleasured exclamations of its audience. But it is quickly gone and forgotten, with no enduring impact. Will we settle for the applause of one great moment of public acclaim? Or will we seek the enduring influence that only comes when one is willing to develop the discipline of a quiet time and a quiet place—to regularly and consistently take time to sit at our Savior's feet to learn from Him?

QUESTIONS FOR REFLECTION AND PRAYER

1. Do you regularly have special times of communion with God, seeking His counsel and instruction? Why or why not? Praise and pray about this right now.

2. When times of conflict come, do you generally turn to the Lord in prayer, or do you try to tough it out on your own? Why? With what results? Ask God now to help you persevere in prayer when you encounter trials.

3. Why are quiet times with God the times He is best able to make you more like His Son, Jesus Christ? Is this happening in your life? Why or why not? Talk to God about your desires in this area right now.

CALLED TO
KEEP PRAYING

"The Scripture abounds

with exhortations

to 'wait on the Lord.'

Instead of becoming impatient,

we should welcome

the opportunity to engage

in a discipline that will

focus attention on the Lord

and develop character in our lives."

4

WHERE
FAITH BEGINS

So then faith comes by hearing,
and hearing by the word of God.

ROMANS 10:17

AS A YOUNG TEENAGER I had the privilege of hearing E. F. "Preacher" Hallock of Norman, Oklahoma. My father was the pastor of our church, and "Preacher" Hallock was the visiting evangelist. I can clearly remember my father sharing with the congregation that "Preacher" Hallock was something of an authority on prayer. I do not recall a great deal of what "Preacher" Hallock said that week, but one observation made a definite impression: "If I had to choose between reading the Bible and praying, I would choose to read the Bible. It is more important for me to hear what God is saying than for God to hear what I am saying." Those words issue a strong warning to those for whom Bible study is less than a priority. Prayer is imperative. But neglect of the Scriptures diminishes its effectiveness.

I heard "Preacher" Hallock speak again later, this time at a week-long youth retreat. "Read God's Word, and ask Him to give you a Bible promise," he emphasized. "No matter what the situation, God has a word for you in His Word." I remember my father gathering our family together and saying, "This man is telling the truth. From now on our family will operate on the principle of Bible promises." Right then I accepted that principle without question.

A few weeks later I prayerfully asked God to give me a Bible promise regarding my life's vocation. He answered through Isaiah 6:8 and made me aware that He was calling me into gospel ministry. It was not until years later that I began to see how important the Word of God is to the ministry of prayer.

The practice of prayer was never intended to be separated from the practice of searching the Scriptures. Jesus said, "If you abide in Me, and My words abide in you, you will ask what you desire, and it shall be done for you" (John 15:7). Effective prayer rests on the authority of God's will as revealed through His Word. And God's Word is best understood by those who prayerfully appeal to Him for discernment.

Sometimes I'm approached by individuals who wish to learn a new method or system for prayer or Bible study. Frustrated on both counts, they are longing for a new insight that will make them want to pray and search the Scriptures. There is no such gimmick. In the end these two practices must be seen as great, worthwhile, and indispensable disciplines of the Christian life that we must choose and maintain with a level of commitment that exceeds emotional desire. It can be said with certainty, however, that if we meet the Lord in the Scriptures, we will long to commune with Him in prayer. And if we meet the Lord in prayer, we will long to walk with Him along Bible pathways. Spending time with God in prayer and in reading His Word are inseparable twins of spiritual life.

A HISTORY LESSON

Man, as God created him, had the remarkable capacity to live in both the physical world and the spiritual world at the same time. God gave him a physical body with its five senses—sight, hearing, smell, taste, and touch. All that man knows about his physical environment, he knows on the basis of information received through those senses. But that is not all there is to man.

Genesis 1:26-27 tells us that man was created in God's "image," and in John 4:24 Jesus taught that "God is Spirit." From this we know that man originally communicated with God on the spiritual level and with the world on a physical level. The first few chapters of Genesis indicate that before falling into sin, Adam and Eve were as sensitive to the voice of God as they were to any of the physical sights or sounds in the Garden of Eden.

The Bible teaches that in addition to the *body*, with which man can communicate in the physical realm, and the *spirit*, with which he can commune with God, he also has a *soul* (sometimes called the "heart"). God thus made it possible for man to choose between following divine instruction or worldly impression. With his soul (intellect, emotion, and will), man can weigh his course of action and make his choices. God created man in this fashion so that a meaningful relationship of love and worship could exist between us and Him. Man's love and obedience would mean little unless there was some capacity *not* to love and obey.

From the beginning Satan, seeking to become "the ruler of this world" (John 12:31), attempted to draw man's allegiance away from God. He appealed to the body ("the woman saw that the tree was good for food, that it was pleasant to the eyes," Gen. 3:6) and the soul ("a tree desirable to make one wise") to convince Eve and then Adam to sin against God. God had said, "Of the tree of the knowledge of good and evil you shall not eat, for in the day that you eat of it you shall surely die" (Gen. 2:17). When Adam and Eve ate from the tree, they died— not in body or soul, but in spirit. They lost their capacity for fellowship with God and their ability to perceive spiritual truth. Sin thus entered the human race and became the inherited nature of all men.

As children of Adam we are all sinful by our very nature (Rom. 3:23). We share the same death experienced by Adam and Eve. We have lost our capacity to commune, or fellowship, with God. The apostle Paul uses the phrase "the natural man" to describe the person who tends to make every decision solely on the basis of physical information and whatever logic or emotion he attaches to it. "But the natural man does not receive the things of the Spirit of God, for they are foolishness to him; neither can he know them, because they are spiritually discerned" (1 Cor. 2:14).

How can a person escape enslavement to the natural world over which Satan has become prince? How can he establish fellowship with God? His only hope is to be born again through the Holy Spirit. Jesus said, "That which is born of the flesh is flesh, and that which is born of the Spirit is spirit. Do not marvel that I said unto you, 'You must be born again'" (John 3:6-7). When a man is spiritually reborn, the Holy Spirit enters his life and reestablishes the fellowship with God that was lost in the Garden of Eden.

THE WORD OR THE WORLD?

With fellowship now a reality, the believer in Christ can walk in sweet communion with his Lord. But that does not mean life is without its challenge from that moment on. The battle begun in the Garden of Eden continues with equal ferocity today as Satan assaults the Christian with information that contradicts the Word of God. Each of us must decide again and again what is true and what is not. Should we believe what the world says or what God's Word says?

The believer who is walking in obedience to Christ is quick to respond, "God's Word is true! That is what I believe, and that is what I will follow!" Unfortunately, the confession of our lips sometimes does not match the behavior of our lives. Bound for heaven, we live as if we are bound to the earth instead—a condition described in 1 Corinthians as "carnal" or "fleshly" (3:1).

When we come to God in prayer, recognizing our weakness and our dependence on Him, He frees us from earthly bondage and places heaven's resources at our disposal. But our prayers must be based upon the truths of God's Word. This is non-negotiable. Jesus said, "If you abide in My word, you are My disciples indeed. And you shall know the truth, and the truth shall make you free" (John 8:31-32). To pray effectively, the believer must settle in his heart that the Word of God is true regardless of what the world says.

Nehemiah stands out in the history of God's people as a great man of prayer. Following a lengthy period of captivity, the Israelites were allowed to return to Jerusalem and rebuild the temple. For years afterward, however, the walls of the great city of God lay in rubble and disarray.

Under the leadership of Nehemiah, against seemingly insurmountable odds, God's people began to rebuild the walls. Nehemiah faced great opposition from every direction. He was laughed at and scorned for his seeming foolishness. His integrity was questioned. Greed, discouragement, and persecution threatened the success of the project. To put it simply, the world was saying, "It cannot be done."

How could Nehemiah find the courage to continue? He was able to keep going because he had searched the Scriptures and had prayed according to the promises of God! "Remember, I pray, the word that You commanded Your servant Moses, saying '. . . I will gather them . . . and bring them to the place which I have chosen as a dwelling for My name'" (Neh. 1:8-9).

Nehemiah had determined that God's Word is true regardless of what the world says. That is the decision we must make if we are to pray effectively.

The Word and Faith

The most difficult part of prayer is not asking but believing. It's difficult to be fully convinced about something we cannot see or know empirically. That is why it is so important for us to recognize and understand what is really true, what we can actually believe. Until we know something is true, we can hope for it, but we cannot believe it, we cannot be certain. Faith is much more than "hoping hard."

Every aspect of our lives should operate by an exercise of faith.

- We are saved by faith (Eph. 2:8-9).
- We live by faith (Gal. 2:20).
- We walk by faith (2 Cor. 5:7).
- We stand by faith (1 Cor. 16:13).
- We overcome obstacles by faith (Matt. 17:20).
- We fight by faith (1 Tim. 6:12).
- We achieve victory by faith (1 John 5:4).

In fact, "Without faith it is impossible to please Him [God]" (Heb. 11:6). The apostle Paul sums it up by saying, "Whatever is not from faith is sin" (Rom. 14:23). But what is faith? What does it mean to believe?

"Now faith is the substance of things hoped for, the evidence of things not seen. For by it the elders obtained a good testimony" (Heb. 11:1-2). Effective prayer is impossible without genuine faith. So it is imperative that we rightly understand what faith is.

FAITH—THE SUBSTANCE OF THINGS HOPED FOR

The word "substance" in Hebrews 11:1 may be accurately translated as "assurance." Further, "faith is the substance of things *hoped* for." But not everything we "hope for" is God's will for us. Faith is the assurance God gives us when our desires (or hopes) are in concert with His will.

How does such assurance come? It comes as God speaks by His Spirit through His Word. Often people will express their desires repeatedly, trying desperately to work up their faith. "I'm just believing he will be healed," I have heard people say of dying loved ones. Then when death occurs, they are puzzled because they were under the impression that they had prayed with faith. Actually they had prayed *hoping* rather than *believing*; they had not received any assurance from God's Word that their loved one would indeed be healed. Faith in the biblical sense is based on the revelation of God's will by His Spirit through His Word.

This element of faith is illustrated interestingly in the fifth chapter of John's gospel. A man beside the pool of Bethesda had suffered with a crippling infirmity for thirty-eight years. Do you think he had ever tried to walk in all those years? Of course! How else did he discover he could not? Do you think he wanted to walk? Certainly! For years he had been brought to the pool, waiting for the miraculous stirring of the water he had heard about. Do you think he hoped one day to be able to walk? Yes! That was why he made repeated attempts to enter the pool at the proper moment. But after thirty-eight years he was apparently convinced that, apart from a miracle, he would never walk; he seemed to have given up. "I have no friends to help me," he complained (see v. 7).

Suppose you had come upon this pitiful figure and asked, "Do you want to be made well?" He would have answered in the affirmative. And suppose you had said, "Then just get up and walk!" You can be assured he would have felt you were having a laugh at his expense. After all, he *couldn't* walk.

But that is precisely how Christ handled the situation. When Christ said, "Rise, take up your bed and walk" (v. 8), faith was born in the heart of that man. Assured that his desire was a reality only waiting to be claimed, he stood up and walked.

What was the basis of this man's faith? Certainly it was not the encouraging words of well-meaning friends. Nor was it based on physical evidence or experience. From those vantage points nothing had changed. *The assurance that his desire was a reality, ready to be claimed, came the moment he heard a word from the Lord.* "Faith comes by hearing, and hearing by the word of God" (Rom. 10:17).

In a similar fashion, when God speaks to us by His Spirit through His Word, "faith" is born in our hearts. That faith gives us the boldness to act with confidence in concert with His will.

FAITH—THE EVIDENCE OF THINGS NOT SEEN

The word "evidence" (Heb. 11:1) may be properly translated as "conviction." While a belief is something you hold, a conviction is something that holds you. You cannot shake loose from a conviction. A paraphrase of this statement might read: "Faith is being convinced that something is real even though you cannot perceive it with your physical senses." This is directly counter to the "seeing is believing" philosophy.

Suppose a college student from the deep South decides to attend his first semester of college in Alaska. He has taken his warmest clothing, but obviously what is sufficient for a southern climate will not keep him warm in Alaska. When the hard, cold winter sets in, his parents, in a rush of concern, buy him an extra-heavy coat and send it by mail. Then they call him to let him know a package is coming.

Standing in an outdoor phone booth, blue with the cold, the student receives his parents' phone call. His father says, "We have sent you a coat." How does his son reply? If he responded to his earthly father in the manner many of us respond to our heavenly Father, the son would continue to beg for the coat. He might go on to state all the reasons he needs it. He might even make numerous additional phone calls to make sure his parents understood his need.

But instead of that response, he simply says, "Thanks." Thanks for what? The coat, of course. He has not seen or felt the coat. But he has the assurance that it is real even though he cannot perceive it with his physical senses. That assurance has come to him because *he believes the word of his father.*

His friends are mystified. "Don't you need a coat?" they ask as he walks through the snow, shivering and red-faced. "No," he says calmly, "I have one!"

Every Christian should have a life-style just as amazing and just as unexplainable in human terms. "Aren't you worried?" others might ask, seeing a certain need in the Christian's life. "No," answers the Christian, "I have what I need." That is how he responds *if* he has a word from his Father.

"Be anxious for nothing." says the Word of God, "but in everything by prayer and supplication, with thanksgiving, let your requests be made known to God" (Phil. 4:6). Thanksgiving is a response of faith when we are convinced the answer is real even though we cannot perceive it with our physical senses.

FAITH—ACTING ON THE REVEALED WILL OF GOD

"For by it [faith] the elders obtained a good testimony" (Heb. 11:2). Whatever else this statement may mean, it includes the acknowledgment that many of God's people in Old Testament times were noted for their faith. This is especially interesting in light of linguistic considerations. The Greek language of the New Testament period expressed many abstract thoughts. A rainstorm, for instance, might be described as the tears of sadness of one of many gods or goddesses. The Hebrew language, on the other hand, which spoke in concrete terms, would describe rain as water falling from the sky. For this reason the Old Testament Hebrew language had no good expression for faith because you could not see it. There were, on the other hand, sufficient expressions for faithfulness because it could be witnessed.

So faith, in the biblical sense, is not merely something we think or feel; it is something we do, something that can be seen. *Faith is acting on the revealed will of God,* obeying what He tells us. As we read the roll call of the faithful in Hebrews 11, we see that none of these individuals were commended for how they felt or for what they thought. They were honored for their actions. They acted on God's will as it was revealed to them.

Many people labor under the tragic misconception that faith is simply believing that God can do anything. Of course He can! But mere acceptance of that fact is not faith in the biblical sense. *Faith is acting on what God has revealed by the Spirit through His Word as His will for our behavior.*

God once told Moses to strike a rock so He could provide water for Israel. Moses acted in faith, struck the rock, and God supplied their need. Later the children of Israel again complained about a lack of water. God could have brought water from the rock in the same manner as before, but this time He instructed Moses to speak to the rock. In anger, however, Moses struck the rock just like before. Moses' unbelief was evidenced by his disobedient behavior. This act of disobedient behavior displeased the Lord and cost Moses his personal entrance into Canaan.

In summary, faith is:

- The assurance that your desire is a reality ready to be claimed.
- The conviction that something is real even though you cannot perceive it with your physical senses.
- Acting on the revealed will of God.

When you have settled that God's Word is true regardless of what the world says, your heart becomes a seed-bed for faith. And when you have faith, you are ready to pray and keep on praying.

QUESTIONS FOR REFLECTION AND PRAYER

1. When you pray, do you generally feel that God is willing to grant your request? That He is *ready* to grant your request? Why or why not? Do your prayers always receive an affirmative response? Why or why not? Discuss these matters with God now.

2. When you feel anxious about personal needs or possible future difficulties, do you usually pray about them? Why or why not? Ask God now to help you be more current in supplication and thanksgiving.

3. Faith is acting on what God has revealed as His will for your behavior, trusting Him fully to be and do what He has promised. Do you find this easy or difficult? Why? Talk to God about this now, requesting greater understanding of His plan for you in specific areas of your life.

5

WHEN GOD'S COUNSEL
IS IGNORED

The men of Israel . . .
did not ask counsel of the LORD.

JOSHUA 9:14

MEN RESPOND IN DIFFERENT WAYS to the gospel message. Some are cut to the heart and cry, "What must I do to be saved?" Others see the sense of it, feel the need of salvation, but stubbornly refuse the grace of God. Still others do not take it seriously at all, considering it a foolish exercise of an overactive imagination.

It is interesting to note that Christians, likewise, respond in different ways to the encouragement to "walk by faith, not by sight" (2 Cor. 5:7). For some there is an immediate acceptance and an eagerness to apply this truth to their lives. Others are reluctant to take the risk of faith. Still others scoff at the idea that God might give instructions pertaining to specific areas of their life. Admittedly, just as there is no way to argue a man into salvation, there is no way to argue a Christian into operating on the basis of God's will as revealed by His Spirit through His Word. It is worth noting, however, the dangers that await those who fail to act in concert with the revealed will of God. Not even such a notable person as Joshua could ignore the counsel of God without severe consequences.

After the death of Moses, Joshua was given the responsibility of leading the Israelites into Canaan and subduing the land. God had

strictly commanded that the Jews make no alliances with the inhabitants of Canaan. After the fall of Jericho and Ai, various kings in
Canaan determined to band their armies together in an attempt to
defeat the Israelites. However, the men of Gibeon refused to join the
Canaanite alliance. Seeing that the power of God was with the
Israelites, yet knowing the Israelites' stubborn refusal to make treaties
with any tribe in Canaan, the Gibeonites devised a subtle plot to draw
the Hebrews into an alliance with them—they pretended to be citizens
of a country far outside Canaan.

Ambassadors dressed in old garments and carrying spoiled food
were sent to the camp of Israel. On the backs of their animals were old
sacks and torn wineskins. Arriving in the Israelite camp at Gilgal, they
said, "We have come from a far country; now therefore make a
covenant with us" (Josh. 9:6). The men of Israel were suspicious at first
and took them to Joshua, who asked, "Who are you, and where do
you come from?" (v. 8). The Gibeonites insisted they had come from
a distant nation because of all they had heard about the power of God
resting upon the Israelites. After being further questioned, they asked
the men of Israel to examine their clothing, food, old sacks, and wineskins. They insisted that all these items were new and fresh when they
had departed from their homeland.

Joshua and his captains were convinced by what they saw and
heard. They "took some of their provisions; but they did not ask counsel of the LORD. So Joshua made peace with them, and made a
covenant with them to let them live; and the rulers of the congregation
swore to them" (vv. 14-15). This was one of the most costly mistakes
in the history of Israel—all because they "did not ask counsel of the
LORD."

FOOLED BY THE WORDS OF MEN

Many unsuspecting Christians have been talked into unholy alliances
because the word of man was their highest counsel. Think how often
you have heard someone say, "He made it sound so good" or "It
wasn't at all like they said it would be." The Christian who fails to seek
God's revealed will through His Word limits his perspective to that of

other men. As such, he is easily misled and frequently falls prey to Satan, who is "a liar and the father of [lies]" (John 8:44).

"From a very far country your servants are come," said the Gibeonites to Joshua, "because of the name of the LORD your God; for we have heard of His fame, and all that He did in Egypt, and all that He did to the two kings of the Amorites who were beyond the Jordan—to Sihon king of Heshbon, and to Og king of Bashan, who was at Ashtaroth. Therefore our elders and all the inhabitants of our country spoke to us, saying, 'Take provisions with you for the journey, and go to meet them, and say unto them, "We are your servants; now therefore, make a covenant with us""" (Josh. 9:9-11). This well-rehearsed plea given to Joshua sounded spiritual, flattering, and humble.

Several years ago God reminded my wife and me that He was interested in every aspect of our lives—even the purchase of a new automobile. Our family was growing, and we were in need of more substantial transportation. After visiting the showrooms of several dealers, we finally decided on the purchase of a basic station wagon. But before we made the purchase I visited a Christian brother who was a member of our church. He told me he was acquainted with a man in the automobile business, and he was sure I could get a good deal from him.

True to our expectations, the dealer showed us a luxury model station wagon and quoted a price several hundred dollars below the cost of the one we had intended to buy. I just knew it was God's will! We were pursuing the advice of a fine Christian man, it was more auto-mobile than we had dreamed of owning, and it cost much less than anticipated (certainly God wanted us to save every penny we could!).

At my wife's encouragement, I agreed to seek God's counsel before making the decision. We asked the Lord to give us guidance through the daily reading of His Word. One morning we were partic-ularly impressed with Proverbs 4:14-15—"Do not enter the path of the wicked, and do not walk in the way of evil. Avoid it, do not travel on it; turn from it and pass on." *Surely*, I thought, *God must be referring to the car we originally intended to purchase*. But in my heart I knew the Lord was referring to the "good deal" we had been offered.

I called the dealer and explained that it was not God's will for us to purchase that automobile. He responded with a few choice words about preachers! We proceeded with settled hearts according to the original plan, though I was a little confused and much disappointed. Several weeks later it became clear that God had rescued us from being swindled! A local newspaper revealed that the man whose offer we had refused had been accused of taking high-mileage automobiles, restoring them to "like new" condition, and selling them to unsuspecting customers. Since then I have often thought of the words of the psalmist who said of the Word of God, "Moreover by them ["the judgments of the LORD"] Your servant is warned" (Ps. 19:11).

FOOLED BY VISIBLE EVIDENCE

Most of us would confess to struggling a long time over a difficult decision only to make the final choice on the basis of flimsy though tangible evidence. For most people, including many Christians, seeing is believing. Since "the sons of this world are more shrewd in their generation than the sons of light" (Luke 16:8), their primary method of operation involves the physical senses. Christians who neglect counsel from God when making decisions often fall victim to worldly or satanic appeals. Eve, for instance, was tempted to sin primarily on this basis. She "*saw* that the tree was *good for food*, that it was *pleasant to the eyes*" (Gen. 3:6). David's great sin began with visual engagement as well (2 Sam. 11:2).

"Look at the evidence," insisted the Gibeonites. "This bread of ours we took hot for our provision from our houses on the day we departed to come to you. But now look, it is dry and moldy. And these wineskins which we filled were new, and see, they are torn; and these our garments and our sandals have become old because of the very long journey" (Josh. 9:12-13). They had carefully contrived visible evidence to make their subtle plot work.

Had Joshua reflected for a moment, he would have recalled that for forty years he and the children of Israel had wandered in the wilderness because they had neglected the Word of God and acted on the basis of a wrongly interpreted visual impression. God had said, "Send men to spy out the land of Canaan, which I am giving to the children of Israel" (Num. 13:2). Having made the search, ten of the spies reported that "the people who dwell in the land are strong; the cities are fortified and very large . . . and we were like grasshoppers in our own sight, and so we were in their sight" (Num. 13:28, 33). Based on this report, the children of Israel had rebelled against God, choosing to walk by sight rather than by faith. If Joshua had remembered that occasion, perhaps he would not have fallen so easily to the Gibeonites' ruse.

How often we need to be reminded that neglecting the Word of God results in being easily fooled by what we see. Joshua should also have recalled the great loss at Ai only a short while before the approach of the Gibeonites. God had allowed them to suffer defeat because one man "*saw* among the spoils a beautiful Babylonian garment, two hundred shekels of silver, and a wedge of gold weighing fifty shekels . . . [and] coveted them and took them" (Josh. 7:21).

It is difficult to live victoriously when much of what we do and own is the result of being easily fooled by what we have heard or seen. Only as we remain in close communication with God through His Word and through the practice of prayer will we avoid being thus deceived.

GOD'S VOICE WITHIN US

God often makes us sensitive to the fact that we are entering a situation in which we need His counsel. If, however, we are determined to handle things on our own, we will ignore those divinely initiated inner reservations.

"Perhaps you dwell among us," said the men of Israel, "so how can we make a covenant with you?" (Josh. 9:7). These comments reveal inner reservations as to the trustworthiness of the Gibeonites. God was encouraging His people to seek His wisdom. But His counsel was ignored, and a treacherous agreement was established.

I remember sharing on this particular subject during a Sunday morning worship service. Afterwards I encountered a man who confessed that on several occasions he had hurriedly bought certain items because he was afraid that, given more time, he might choose not to make the purchase! In virtually every case the decision had brought him great distress. The world often says, "If you buy now, you'll get a better deal than if you buy later." But God sometimes urges us to wait, and no matter how the situation might appear to us, we should listen to Him.

Satan often uses time pressures to lure us into wrong actions. But God is the creator of time, and we measure time by the things God has created (the revolution of the earth on its axis, etc.). Consequently, *time is on the side of the person who is on the side of God*. The Christian who waits upon the Lord for His guidance and leadership, accepting His timing, can be assured that God will always provide a way to do what He commands us to do. As we will see later, God even made time stand still so Joshua could gain victory in a battle that resulted from his misguided alliance with the Gibeonites.

I frequently hear from persons who are experiencing problems in marriage. "I must confess," they sometimes say, "that I had some reservations prior to our marriage." Some even go so far as to admit they were firmly convinced the relationship would *not* last. But since the invitations were sent and a cancellation would be embarrassing, they forged ahead, ignoring inner urgings from God to call off the wedding. Certainly God is able to counsel us regarding the kind of behavior that will bring peace into a marriage. But better yet, many broken homes would be averted if couples waited for a clear understanding of God's will prior to marriage. Accepting His guidance as to whether or not to marry or when to marry is always best.

Similar situations often develop in church-staff relationships. Individuals who usually affirm they were brought together by the Lord respond differently when trouble is brewing. Once they are in the middle of stormy circumstances, they confess to having experienced inner reservations from the beginning. Everything looked and sounded so right; they were sure God would give peace of heart and mind once they began serving together. But that just did not happen! How different things might have been had both parties waited upon the Lord for divine guidance through His Word.

When the Lord indicates we should wait for further guidance, it is imperative to follow the advice of Proverbs 3:5-6: "Trust in the

LORD with all your heart, and *lean not on your own understanding*. In all your ways acknowledge Him, and He shall direct your paths." Through prayer and the study of God's Word, we can seek the mind of God. A reluctance to discover His will indicates either an exaggerated self-confidence or the fear that God will not endorse our selfish desires. We should avoid these errors at all costs.

THE COST OF COMMITMENT TO THE WORLD

If we persist in our refusal to seek counsel from God, we will ultimately make a costly commitment to the world. "Then the men of Israel took some of their provisions; but they did not ask counsel of the LORD. So Joshua made peace with them, and made a covenant with them to let them live" (Josh. 9:14-15). Israel was now engaging in open disobedience to the will of God, and this mistake was costly.

Within three days the Israelites discovered that the Gibeonites were, in fact, their neighbors. Bound to keep their word, God's people were committed to provide for their enemies' safety. Adopting a middle position, the Israelites decided that the Gibeonites would be servants—"woodcutters and water carriers for all the congregation" (Josh. 9:21). One might imagine that the Israelites smugly assumed they had turned a sinful commitment into a beneficial arrangement. However, they soon discovered otherwise.

Several of the kings of Canaan, fearful of the power of the Israelites, determined to attack them at what was now their weakest point, the city of Gibeon. At the height of the battle the Gibeonites sent a message to Joshua, camped at Gilgal: "Do not forsake your servants; come up to us quickly, save us and help us, for all the kings of the Amorites who dwell in the mountains have gathered together against us" (Josh. 10:6). When Joshua's soldiers should have been preparing for the systematic conquest of Canaan, they were instead marching off to protect a city of slaves!

When we ignore the counsel of God through a prayerful searching of His Word, we will ultimately make costly commitments to the world. Notice the price of such commitments:

They give Satan a point of attack. A young executive accepted a position with his company because it "looked so good, I couldn't afford to turn it down." He made no attempt to discern the will of God in the situation. "Now," he confessed, "I find myself compromising my convictions just to gain a contract. I am failing as a husband, father, and Christian because I am unable to withstand the constant temptations." His giving in to the world opened the way for Satan's attack.

The Israelites' compromise by making a treaty with the Gibeonites put them in danger. Because Gibeon was such a vulnerable city, the attention of the enemy naturally went to it. In the same way, the Christian who ignores the counsel of God when making an important decision (job, dating relationship, investment or purchase, etc.) makes himself vulnerable to Satan's attack on specific points.

Such commitments to the world will beg for our attention. Joshua was assembling his troops and planning strategy at Gilgal when the message came: "Come up to us quickly, save us and help us." This was not a convenient addition to Joshua's schedule. But the Israelites had made a commitment to the Gibeonites, and now they had to be faithful to their word. Commitments made to the world, though not ideal or spiritually prudent, will require follow-up responses of faithfulness and honesty, responses that make demands on our time and on our hearts.

Once I purchased an automobile because of its reputation for dependability. The Lord subtly reminded me that I should pray and seek His leadership. But I was sure I couldn't go wrong with such a fine car. However, for the following year and a half my "dependable" automobile was constantly in the shop. Since then I have talked with others who made similar commitments, whether for work or pleasure, with similar results. That is what happens when we obligate ourselves to the world.

Commitments to the world deplete your resources. Joshua's men routed the army of the Amorites, but to do so, they expended an enormous amount of energy and time in a way other than originally planned. Commitments to the world always exhaust our assets—physically, spiritually, financially, emotionally. I have known fine Christians who lost huge sums of money while trying to strike it rich. Resources that might have been used to win many to Christ were lost needlessly.

The prophet Haggai said of those who ignore the counsel of God,

"Consider your ways! You have sown much, and bring in little; you eat, but do not have enough; you drink, but you are not filled with drink; you clothe yourselves, but no one is warm; and he who earns wages, earns wages to put into a bag with holes" (Hag. 1:5-6). We too need to consider our ways and examine our commitments. Are our resources being depleted by commitments to the world and a refusal to ask God for His wisdom and direction? The neglect of prayer carries a huge price!

RECOVERING OUR WALK OF FAITH

What an error it is to walk by sight rather than by faith, to believe what we perceive with our physical senses more readily than that which the Lord reveals through His Word! The inevitable results of such an error are a series of commitments to the world and the loss of the freedom that comes from obeying God. Are you involved in misplaced commitment at this time? Can victory and effectiveness be restored in your life? Joshua discovered that a commitment made to the world must be given to God if triumph is ever to be regained.

By making servants of the Gibeonites, the Israelites thought they had turned bad into good. Their attempt, however, resulted in the added obligation of protecting those who were actually their enemies. They soon discovered that only God can make "all things work together for good to those who love God, to those who are the called according to His purpose" (Rom. 8:28).

As Joshua marched his troops from Gilgal to Gibeon, the Lord spoke to him. And this time Joshua listened and obeyed. "And the LORD said to Joshua, 'Do not fear them, for I have delivered them into your hand; not a man of them shall stand before you.' Joshua *therefore* came upon them suddenly, having marched all night from Gilgal" (Josh. 10:8-9).

It was on this occasion that the Lord performed one of the greatest miracles in history, causing the sun and moon to stand still at the command of Joshua. "And there has been no day like that, before it or after it, that the LORD heeded the voice of a man; for the LORD fought for Israel" (Josh. 10:14). Then followed the successful campaign that allowed the entire southern portion of Canaan to be taken by the Israelites.

We learn a simple but important lesson here: If we have made a commitment to the world because we ignored the counsel of God, we must repent and turn back to God and seek His counsel regarding the measures He wants us to take to achieve victory.

If we do now what we failed to do at first, God's method of deliverance might be recorded as one of the greatest miracles of our lives!

QUESTIONS FOR REFLECTION AND PRAYER

1. In what ways are you sometimes tempted to believe foolish words of men rather than the ever-trustworthy Word of God? Why are you susceptible to such an error? What can you do to avoid it? Discuss this in detail with God now.

2. What kinds of visible evidence sometimes divert you from God's path for your life? Why is such evidence at times more appealing than spending time with God and seeking His counsel? Pray for understanding and enlightenment right now.

3. What commitments to the world have you made that made you vulnerable to Satan's attacks? With what results? Have you confessed these and returned to God? With what results? Talk to God about all this now.

6

WHEN THE WORD
IS IN OUR HEART

*"For then you will make
your way prosperous, and then you
will have good success."*

JOSHUA 1:8

ARE THERE DIFFERENCES between success and effectiveness? Depending, of course, on how you define these terms, the differences can be great. Our world would have us believe that success is everything. We are told how to plan for it, achieve it, measure it, dress for it, advertise it, and enjoy it! But those who have "arrived" will tell us in moments of sober reflection that such success is not all it is cracked up to be.

Like cotton candy, success looks impressive and tastes great for a while. But it is more form than substance, and soon it is gone, with nothing remaining but a bothersome residue. It is not always easy to clean up after worldly success—to restore broken relationships, recapture trust, and renew vision.

Effectiveness, on the other hand, is measured in terms of impact. It is a matter of investing the resources of your life (your energy, time, intellect, ability, etc.) in a way that will accomplish goals carrying significant spiritual and human value. A stick of dynamite can be successfully detonated in an empty field. But strategically placed in a rock quarry, the detonation can be both successful and effective.

A SPIRITUAL KEY

What is the primary secret to effectiveness in any believer's life? *Consistently spending time with the Lord in His Word each day.* This may sound like an oversimplification, but it is essential for spiritual living. Every area of our lives must be built on the Word of God. Our effectiveness in prayer will especially depend largely upon the time we spend in God's Word.

As I mentioned earlier, I am deeply indebted to the teachings of E. F. "Preacher" Hallock, who pastored the First Baptist Church in Norman, Oklahoma, for many years before his retirement. "Preacher" was a man who lived by the promises of God's Word. For him, prayer was a matter of finding God's will in His Word and coming to God's terms on the basis of what he found there. He had discovered the secret of effectiveness.

Several years ago I was invited to play golf at one of the world's most prestigious courses. (Believe me, I did *not* receive the invitation because of my golfing abilities.) On that course there is a hole that ranks as one of the most famous in the world. It is part of a series of holes that a frustrated golfer once nicknamed the "Amen Corner." (When you've finished, you feel like shouting "Amen" in relief!) When I was pondering a lay-up shot to that green (a short, easy, no-risk shot), my caddie exclaimed, "You didn't fly all the way from Oklahoma to hit a lay-up at the Amen Corner!"

Spiritual lessons, I suppose, have been taught in stranger places. But he was right, about the golf shot *and* life. God does not intend for us to go through life merely hitting lay-ups. He wants us to strive for excellence, to be *effective*, to be all we can be with His enablement.

Joshua made this discovery one life-changing day. The mantle of responsibility shouldered by Moses for forty years now rested on him. This was no time for a lay-up. He wanted to know how he could effectively lead Israel into the Promised Land, and God clearly revealed to him the great secret of effectiveness:

> *"This Book of the Law shall not depart from your mouth, but you shall meditate in it day and night, that you may observe to do according to all that is written in it. For then you will make*

your way prosperous, and then you will have good success [effectiveness]."

—JOSHUA 1:8

What was God really saying to Joshua about the relationship between effectiveness and time spent in His Word? How can we today make a practice of consistently feeding on the Word of God? These are important matters for the individual who desires effectiveness in prayer.

TOP PRIORITY

When I was just a young boy, my father taught me how to ride a bicycle. With legs barely long enough to reach the pedals, I took a wobbly start on an exercise that would provide literally thousands of hours of pleasure in the years ahead. I can still remember my dad running alongside and shouting words of encouragement: "Look up! Don't look down! Look far down the road!" Later, when my father taught me to drive a car, I heard those same words again: "Look on down the road! Pick a spot way out front, and you won't keep veering back and forth!" He knew that a long view would help me avoid the jerkiness resulting from reacting to the things immediately surrounding me.

God cautioned Joshua to avoid the kind of reactionary living that results from giving greater attention to the human viewpoint than to the divine. He wanted to deliver Joshua from a distracted existence that results from short-sighted goals. Joshua was urged to take the long view, and in order to do so he needed to focus more on the Word than on the world.

THE WORD AND OUR CONSIDERATION

We must give the Word of God primary consideration if we are to be effective. "Meditate in [consider] it day and night," says the Lord. This means, first of all, that we are to surround ourselves with the Word of God. It is imperative that we read it, memorize it, meditate on it, obey it.

The psalmist said that the "blessed" man meditates on "the law of the Lord." He is like "a tree *planted* by *the rivers* of water, that *brings forth its fruit* in its season, whose leaf also shall *not wither*; and whatever he does *shall prosper*" (Ps. 1:1-3). What an exciting definition of an effective life!

We must also saturate ourselves with the Word of God—"day and night." Occasionally I turn on our lawn sprinkler, then become preoccupied with other tasks and fail to turn it off. The next morning I find the lawn so saturated with water that every place I step, water oozes to the surface. Our intake of the Word should be so frequent and so thorough that life's pressures yield a godly response consistent with God's Word.

For almost twenty-five years now I have included the reading of a chapter of Proverbs as part of my daily Bible study. I am amazed at how often the exigencies of life bring to mind a verse from Proverbs that serves to guide my behavior and my choices. In the same way, I often recall biblical models who provide me with spiritual leadership during times of critical decision-making.

A friend of mine who employs a similar practice in Bible reading recently determined that he would seek to redeem his fellow employees rather than retaliate for their unethical behavior. He said he was inspired by Joseph's response to his brothers. This shows that he was saturated with the Word of God.

THE WORD AND OUR CONVERSATION

"Be wise when you listen to others," my mother used to say, "because what a person talks about a little, he thinks about a lot!" Or as our Lord said, "Out of the abundance of the heart the mouth speaks" (Matt. 12:34). Ultimately your mouth will tell on you! God knew that Joshua's conversation would either strengthen or weaken his effectiveness, so he stressed, "This Book of the Law shall not depart from your mouth" (Josh. 1:8). An alternate rendering of that phrase is, "Your conversation must be filled with the Word of God."

Several years ago I visited briefly with a man whom God had used in a significant way to bring revival to his native country. I remarked to my wife that listening to him speak was like listening to the Bible on cassette recording. Every sentence, it seemed, was filled with Scripture either by intimation or direct quotation. Later, as I listened to a message preached by the same man, I noted that over half its content was quoted from Scripture! Little wonder that his ministry was so effective!

When God told Joshua, "This Book of the Law shall not depart from your mouth," He was saying, "My Word must be the subject of your speech." *If we give primary consideration to the Word of God, our conversation will be filled with the Word of God.*

God's Word must also be the *seasoning* for our speech. A good cook knows the value of proper flavoring. Food that is properly seasoned creates the desire for more. *If your conversation is to bear fruit, it must be so seasoned with the Word of God that others will receive it and want more.* My grandfather once said, "Your messages should be so scriptural that if people have an argument, it is with God rather than with you."

God says that *our speech must be screened by the Word of God.* In other words, nothing should escape our lips that will not pass the test of God's Word. I sometimes envision the tablets of the law positioned in front of my mouth. Before speaking, I should ask if what I am about to say is consistent with the Scriptures. Will my words be acceptable and approved by God? When tempted, for instance, to speak in a harsh, retaliating fashion I should recall that "a soft answer turns away wrath" (Prov. 15:1).

THE WORD AND OUR CONDUCT

Being precedes doing. What a man *is*, he ultimately *does.* This is why instruction and discipline are wasted on a foolish man. "As a dog returns to his vomit, so a fool repeats his folly" (Prov. 26:11). A fool always ends up doing what he is.

Who can forget Saul's sad commentary on a life that could have been? "I have played the fool and erred exceedingly" (1 Sam. 26:21). How can you avoid such tragedy in your own life? How can you use the gifts God has given you more effectively? Only by spending time in the Word of God—". . . that you may observe to do according to all that is written."

Your behavior should be chosen on the basis of God's Word. This is why God reminded Joshua that he was to spend time in the Word, so he could "observe to do." He was to give serious thought to his behavior, and so are we. Virtually every self-inflicted problem in our lives results from a failure to seriously reflect on Scripture *before* acting.

A friend of mine fell head over heels in love with a beautiful girl at the college he attended. Ignoring God's caution that believers should not be "unequally yoked together with unbelievers" (2 Cor. 6:14), he ardently pursued the relationship, assuming that "at the right moment" he could lead her to Christ. Instead, she led him—into premarital sex, into a strife-filled marriage made even more painful by her adultery, into a divorce, and out of a promising ministry. "I only wish I had observed the counsel of God's Word," he later lamented. He had failed to take the long view available to those who consistently spend time in the Word of God. His carnal heart had greater control of his life than did heaven.

God is saying, "If you want to be effective, you must think about your conduct. What will be the consequences of your behavior? Where will your current choices ultimately take you?" To neglect these crucial matters is worse than jumping out of an airplane without a parachute.

Your behavior must be consistent with the whole counsel of God's Word. God tells us to "observe to do *according to all that is written.*" Time spent in the Word of God will prevent us from selectively following some biblical principles but ignoring other divine counsel that is equally significant. Balance is a key to effectiveness in the Christian life. Major religious sects have been born in the hearts of individuals who have gone overboard on certain issues while ignoring the counsel of God's law in general.

There were times in Israel's history when immorality was rampant. They rationalized their behavior, however, by pointing to the frequency of their sacrifices. God sent prophets to remind them that they should not practice a selective faith. They were to give attention to their conduct as well as to their sacrifices. In fact, they were to learn, as Samuel told Saul, that "to obey is better than sacrifice" (1 Sam. 15:22). Listen to the prophet Micah as well:

> *Will the LORD be pleased with thousands of rams, ten thousand rivers of oil? Shall I give my firstborn for my transgression, the fruit of my body for the sin of my soul? He has shown you, O man, what is good; and what does the LORD require of you but to do justly, to love mercy, and to walk humbly with your God?*
>
> —MICAH 6:7-8

Only by spending sufficient time in the Word of God can we learn to behave in a manner that is consistent with His counsel.

A church member, excited over his experience at a conference he had attended, came to visit with me about "a spiritual matter." As it turned out, he actually had come by to reprimand both his church and its leadership for what he termed a "lack of spiritual depth as evidenced by the failure to express a certain gift." "You will never really experience growth in the Lord," he went on, "until you begin exercising this gift." He then explained the "gift" he had received at the conference.

Without challenging his theology, I questioned him about the impact of this experience on his life. Because we were friends and I was his pastor, I raised some serious questions about other areas of conduct in his life, such as his lack of biblical stewardship, his unwillingness to witness, his poor attendance at church, and his refusal to accept a ministry responsibility. I then asked him how much time he spent in God's Word each day. "All that emphasis on the Bible leaves me cold. I want to really practice my Christianity!" he responded. His failure to spend time regularly in the Word had led to the selective practice of God's principles.

It is easy but dangerous to measure our spirituality and the spirituality of others on the basis of something less than "all that is written." The evidence of gifts can become more significant than the existence of the Giver. We can exalt diet over duty, dress over devotion, work over witness, music over motive, form over function—

the list is endless. Instead, may we put God first, and demonstrate that by consistently spending time with Him in His Word and in prayer.

GOD'S COUNSEL

God was concerned about Joshua's effectiveness as a leader. Joshua was, after all, Moses' successor. What sandals he had to fill! The Lord was concerned lest Joshua become a leader who majored on minors, a leader who lost sight of the big picture and failed to accomplish all that God was willing to do through him. And so He shared with him the single greatest secret of effectiveness in the believer's life: *No practice can take the place of daily time spent in His Word.* Even our prayer life will be cold and meaningless without this spiritual discipline.

Can you hear God's words to Joshua echoing in your own heart? If you are not already doing so, will you begin now to set aside time each day for diligent attention to the Word of God? Find a place, get it ready, set a time, and keep your appointment!

God desires to share the depths of His heart with you. Are you willing to meet with Him?

QUESTIONS FOR REFLECTION AND PRAYER

1. How does giving God's Word top priority affect our lives practically day by day? Are you giving the Word supreme consideration? How can you tell? Praise and pray about this now.

2. Is your conversation generally seasoned and screened by the Word of God? Does your speech need to be even more impacted by the Scriptures? Why or why not? Talk to God about this in specific terms right now.

3. Are you submitting your life to the whole counsel of God, or are you engaging in selective obedience? If the latter, why are you doing this, and what does God want you to do to correct the situation? Discuss this with God now.

7

PRAYING A MATTER THROUGH!

. . . if we ask anything according to
His will, He hears us.

1 JOHN 5:14

THERE IS A SIMPLICITY at the heart of the Christian life that is often missed in discussions by more technical analysts or commentators. I submit the thoughts in this chapter (and indeed the entire book) with the prayer that you will not become more intrigued with a system than with this simple fact: "As you therefore have received Christ Jesus the Lord, so walk in Him" (Col. 2:6). Those few words state the pattern of operation for every aspect of the Christian life, including the discipline of prayer.

Consider how we each entered into a saving relationship with Jesus Christ. While our circumstances may differ, our experiences share certain similarities. For that reason I am sure you can identify with the elements of my own conversion.

As a young boy I came under the deep conviction that the awful presence of sin in my life was making fellowship with God impossible. Since the issue was my relationship with God, I knew I must go to Him for the solution. God, in turn, spoke to me by His Spirit through His Word.

In my particular case the setting was a discussion with my parents following an outdoor crusade at our local church. As a "preacher's kid," I had heard that great salvation verse, John 3:16, on hundreds of previous occasions. But that night, more aware than ever of my need, God's Spirit brought the verse to life, and I received it as a message from God to me. Accepting God's Word as true, I confessed my faith in Jesus Christ, believing that He would enter my heart, take away my sin, and reign as my Lord. I believed in Him, and He, according to His promise, granted the salvation that I now joyfully confess as mine.

Your encounter with Christ undoubtedly differs from mine in certain respects, but our conversions share several elements in common. Colossians 2:6 teaches that the elements of "conversion experience" make up a pattern for the entire Christian life, including the practice of prayer. These elements are: (1) acknowledging our need; (2) talking to God; (3) God's revelation of His will through His Word; (4) our receiving His Word as true and responding in faith; (5) God's hearing and answering. Note how these elements appear in effective prayer.

A great prayer promise is found in 1 John 5:14-15: "Now this is the confidence that we have in Him, that if we ask anything according to His will, He hears us. And if we know that He hears us, whatever we ask, we know that we have the petitions that we asked of Him." In other words, *the key to answered prayer is asking according to the will of God*. The following steps will help us do just that!

Step 1: Acknowledging Our Need

Every believer must come to grips with the fact that he is intimately related to the one who reigns as the supreme God. This biblical truth is especially difficult for those who, knowingly or unknowingly, pit man's freedom against God's sovereignty. *Both doctrines are taught in the Scriptures; both doctrines stand true*. The fact that we cannot comprehend everything about the way God has chosen to operate does not erase the truth of these teachings or hinder their operation.

Since God is sovereign, some words are *not* a part of His vocabulary. God never says, "Oops!" or "I didn't know that!" or "That one sure slipped up on me!" To believe in a sovereign God is to agree that every circumstance of life is known by God *before* it occurs and that, for whatever reason, He has not chosen to alter its course. We cannot justly find fault with His choices in these matters.

But aren't some problems caused by Satan? The book of Job is sufficient evidence that God is even the God of the Devil, who could not do a single thing against Job unless God allowed him to. God's sovereignty is a great encouragement to all Christians, for "we know that all things work together for good to those who love God, to those who are the called according to His purpose" (Rom. 8:28).

Unfortunately, most Christians do not view their problems or needs in the proper perspective. Imagine, for instance, that a difficult situation knocks on the door of your life. Perhaps it is threatened job loss or a health problem or financial reverses. How will you respond? Will you cower in fear or rant in anger or adopt a victim mentality? Or will you fall on your knees and ask God to be your strength and your deliverer? Will you honestly talk with Him about the situation and your fear or anxieties? A focus on self or on God—that is the crucial choice.

After losing his health, wealth, family, and friends, Job lamented, "The thing I greatly feared has come upon me" (Job 3:25). Apparently Satan takes good notes when we confess our fears. He eavesdrops and observes, then initiates a battle plan against us. But of course God is also aware of the situation and is ready to come to our defense and deliverance. Why do we speak and act as if some needs are too great for God to handle?

In one sense we should welcome difficulties, recognizing that our Lord can use them to make us stronger and to bring us closer to Him. As we encounter trials of various kinds, we need to keep certain considerations in mind.

Through our problems God can prove to the world how powerfully He provides for His people. The greater the need, the greater the testimony to God's grace, and often, by God's design, the greater the audience.

Through our problems God is making available to us blessings for which we have not asked. He is allowing us to face difficulties so we will ask for and accept that which He wants us to have for our welfare and His glory.

Through our problems God is reminding us that we are still in His school of prayer. The Scriptures tell us repeatedly that God's provision comes in answer to petition and intercession. The needs of our lives today are part of God's plan to keep us praying.

Our problems are a call to worship. That was Job's immediate response to all that befell him. Is it ours? We each would do well to make a list of our needs, then let the world and the Devil see how powerful God is as we attach new meanings to our troubles and praise our awesome God in every situation, no matter how troubling or taxing.

STEP 2: TURNING TO GOD FOR THE ANSWER

"Take it to the Lord in prayer." That frequently stated advice is usually met with, "Of course! I always do that!" However, for many Christians, God is a last resort. Most of us, when we encounter some need, want to solve the problem ourselves. "I'll go see another doctor." "Perhaps I should contact my pastor." "Maybe my friend will have some helpful advice." "Perhaps if I ignore the situation it will go away." "A good counselor will probably have the right answer." Finally, if none of these bring adequate assistance, we cry out, "Dear God . . . help!"

Granted, God's answer *might* be found by seeking advice from a friend or waiting for the difficulty to take care of itself. But it is a waste of time to pursue any course of action until God has specifically directed us to do so. Prayer first, not last, is always the best course of action.

Ephesians 6:12 reminds us that "we do not wrestle against flesh and blood, but against principalities, against powers, against the rulers of the darkness of this age, against spiritual forces of wickedness in the heavenly places." In other words, our warfare is not merely a "flesh and blood" or physical issue. This is why the problems in our lives should trigger immediate consultation with the Lord. "Father, what is Your will concerning this situation?" Only His answer to our needs is enough.

STEP 3: DISCOVERING GOD'S REVEALED WILL

The Bible, an inerrant record of God's dealings with men, reveals that He has spoken "at various times and in various ways" (Heb. 1:1). Thus it would be foolish to say that God *always* or *only* speaks to us in a certain manner. On the other hand, the Bible does clearly indicate the basic fashion in which He reveals His will to us—by His Spirit, through His Word.

In 1 Corinthians 2:9-10, 12 the apostle Paul emphasizes the role of the Holy Spirit in revealing the will of God. He begins by saying, "But as it is written, 'Eye has not seen, nor ear heard, nor have entered into the heart of man the things which God has prepared for those who love Him'" (v. 9). Clearly, "things God has prepared for us" are not physically sensed or intellectually contrived.

Paul continues, however, by stating that "God has revealed them to us through His Spirit. For the Spirit searches all things, yes, the deep things of God" (v. 10). And to this he adds the joyous reminder: "Now we have received, not the spirit of the world, but the Spirit who is from God, *that we might know* the things that have been freely given to us by God" (v. 12).

But how does the Holy Spirit speak to the believer? Though God uses many methods of communicating with us, He has assured us there is one way He will always speak to us—*through His Word, the Bible.* The apostle Paul was referring to that fact when he wrote to Timothy, "All Scripture is given by inspiration of God [i.e., it is God-breathed], and is profitable for doctrine, for reproof, for correction, for instruction in righteousness, that the man of God may be complete, thoroughly equipped for every good work" (2 Tim. 3:16-17).

"*All* Scripture," Paul is saying, "provides *all* a Christian needs to know in order to be and do all that God desires for him or her." Seeing our need, the Holy Spirit takes the precious truths of Scripture and applies them to our hearts. Those truths constitute the living word— the word God speaks.

A consideration of the original language of the New Testament illustrates how God's Spirit speaks through His Word to reveal His will. The Greek word *logos* (used in John 1:1 and other Scriptures) describes a tangible expression of thought such as a written word. *Rhema*, on the other hand, was used to describe a personal spoken expression. For instance, in Ephesians 6:11-17 the Christian is told to put on various pieces of armor for spiritual warfare, and in verse 17 he is encouraged to fight with "the sword of the Spirit, which is the word of God." Here "word" is *rhema*. "The sword of the Spirit" is the truth God "personalizes" for you by His Spirit as you read the Word of God.

How exciting it is to know that God stands ever ready to reveal His will to us by His Spirit through His Word. At the same time, there are prerequisites to hearing what God is saying. This is why the next step is so crucial.

STEP 4: UNDERSTANDING AND RECEIVING GOD'S WORD

To communicate adequately, people must speak and listen in the same language. This is equally true of our communication with God. If God is speaking by His Spirit through His Word, *only the individual living in the fullness of the Spirit and engaged in consistent study of the Word can discern God's will.*

Jesus said, "If you abide in Me, and My words abide in you, you will ask what you desire, and it shall be done for you" (John 15:7), thus linking the filling of the Spirit and consistent time in the Word with the practice of prayer. To "abide" in Christ is synonymous with living in the fullness of the Spirit—to settle down or make our home entirely within the boundaries of Christ—to consistently live life in light of who He is and what He asks of His people. Abiding in Christ means having no rebellion in our hearts toward the Lord or His will for our lives—living in complete surrender to His Lordship.

Some Christians see themselves as forced servants, trapped against their will by one who denies them their desires. This is not abiding in Christ, because the heart is in rebellion. But when a Christian gladly acknowledges that he has changed his citizenship and joyfully submits himself to his new Lord, he is abiding in Christ, serving wholeheartedly with abounding joy.

Notice, however, that abiding in Christ is only the first issue. Jesus also states that *His words must abide in us*. The Bible must be at home in our lives. This implies consistent, habitual Bible reading and study; there is nothing sporadic about abiding.

Occasionally a desperate Christian will throw open his Bible, jam his finger onto the page, and attempt to receive spiritual light from whatever verse he finds there. This is *not* the habit our Lord is encouraging for the believer who continually wants God's wisdom. Only a day-by-day study of God's Word will suffice.

Some Christians scoff at the idea that God's will about specific situations can be found through His Word. They suggest that the Bible contains only general or guiding principles useful in developing a Christian approach to life. God is, indeed, a God of principle, but He also longs to walk beside us in intimate and loving fellowship. Such fellowship means that God takes seriously all individual matters about which we are concerned or anxious—every felt need. As we walk with Him in intimate fellowship, He applies His principles to the issues that confront us, showing us how to respond in faith.

Some feel that finding the will of God in the Word of God is too subjective. But when asked what method they propose for determining God's plan for them, they generally indicate a procedure that involves a little gathering of information, a bit of prayer, and then playing their hunch. Now, *that* is subjective!

Others state that God simply reveals His will through open or closed doors. Sometimes He does. But remember, the Devil can arrange circumstances too. Looking for an open door is not the most reliable method of recognizing the Lord's will. An open door might be God's guidance, or it might be a satanic trap leading to paths of destruction (see Prov. 14:2).

Please do not misunderstand me. Gathering information about an issue *is* useful; having a settled peace in our hearts *is* important; open doors *can* indeed indicate God's desire in a certain matter. But none of these practices should take the place of *consistent study of God's Word along a prescribed pattern (whatever plan of Bible study we may use)*. Through this exercise we will learn His principles *and* sense His heart.

Remember, no mere plan will make us want to study the Scriptures. To overcome apathy about Bible reading, we must *choose to read the Word of God for the express purpose of meeting the Lord and having personal fellowship with Him*. This must be more than a frantic searching for His will. Through reading His Word, we will begin to develop a deep sense of communion with God. We will discover that fellowship with Him is more important than knowing what to do. We must seek His heart rather than merely His endorsement of our plans.

How will we know when we have found God's revealed will regarding the specific need about which we are praying? Knowing is the result of God's speaking by His Spirit through His Word to our surrendered heart. "As you therefore have received Christ Jesus the Lord, so walk in Him" (Col. 2:6). Our lives as believers should be consistent with our receiving Christ as our Savior, and that consistency will assure we do indeed belong to God. In the same way that the Holy Spirit revealed to us the truth of the Gospel in God's Word (1 John 4:13), He also bears witness that a specific passage of Scripture is His prescription for our problem, His guide for our behavior.

One day I was asked about this issue of *knowing* whether something is a genuine revelation of God's will. God gave me a phrase that I have used often since then: *A Bible promise is not a verse we grab; it is a verse that grabs us* as, within the context of our need, we surrender our lives to a consistent study of the Scriptures. It is imperative to remember that God will never give us freedom to operate in a manner that is inconsistent with the prinicples of Scripture.

STEP 5: MAKING A FAITH REQUEST

If we have determined that God's Word is true, regardless of what the world says, and if God has directed us regarding a specific situation, then our part is simply to agree with Him and do His bidding. In this way we enter into aggressive cooperation with God's revealed will. First John 5:14–15 tells us that confident prayer depends on asking according to His will. We agree with God by requesting that His will be done on earth as we have discerned it by looking into heaven.

> And this is the confidence that we have in Him, that if we ask anything according to His will, he hears us: and if we know that He hears us, whatever we ask, we know that we have the petitions that we have asked of Him.

Suppose you decide to give your child a bicycle for Christmas. Perhaps you have in fact already purchased it, and now it is stored in the attic. But you want to encourage your child to ask for what you want to give him.

"Son," you say, "what would you like for Christmas?" "Electric trains," he might reply. Since this is not the answer you desire, you begin to point out the merits of bicycle ownership and the joy that comes from riding a bike, thus encouraging him to want what you know will be profitable for him.

At Christmas approaches, you begin to become concerned because your son has not yet agreed with your plans for him. Finally he says, "You know, I've been doing a lot of thinking about what you've said. I believe you're right. Dad, I sure would like a bicycle."

What does he receive? Exactly what he asked for!

This illustration helps us begin to understand what praying in faith is all about. We find God's will and then pray in concert with it and act upon it, knowing God always wants what is best for us.

The Scriptures tell us both to "pray without ceasing" (1 Thess. 5:17) *and* to pray specific, one-time prayers of commitment (see, for example, Ps. 37:4-5). Some imagine a conflict here, but the prayer without ceasing is the prayer you pray *until* you find the revealed will of God. Abraham's intercession for Lot in Genesis 18:23-33 (see the discussion of this passage in Chapter 1) is a good example. Once we find the revealed will of God, we must simply commit ourselves to Him and act according to His prescribed course. If we pray again about the matter, it is simply to express gratitude for His involvement in the situation regardless of how things appear to be working out.

Once we have made our faith request, agreeing to enter into active cooperation with God's will, we are ready to experience the final, exciting step of effective prayer.

STEP 6: THANKING GOD FOR ANSWERED PRAYER

On one occasion I found myself swept along in a great moving of God's Spirit because of a promise God had made to a young woman who was praying for her father. This came about while several men were gathered for a prayer meeting in our church. As we prayed I heard the office phone begin to ring. There was such a persistence about the ringing that I finally slipped out of the prayer meeting, made my way to the office, and lifted the receiver. I was surprised to hear the voice of a college friend I had not seen for several years.

My friend explained that she was working at a halfway house on the California coast. Then she explained the reason for her call. She had met and ministered to a young woman who had since returned to her home in a western state. As a new Christian, the young woman had become burdened for her friends and family, especially for her father. God had given her a scriptural assurance that he would bring revival to her hometown, and she was acting on His promise. She had secured the use of the high school gymnasium for a three-day period. Then, at a loss as to what to do next, she called my friend for advice. They agreed to ask a preacher to come and hold services. "Will you come?" asked my friend.

I assured her that I was sympathetic with what was happening, but since there seemed to be a lack of local church sponsorship, and since the meeting was only two weeks away, I would be unable to come. "Pray about it," she insisted, "and call me later." I agreed, but I was sure I would not be able to accommodate her request.

I returned to the prayer meeting and related the incident to the men. They responded in a remarkable fashion, especially considering the negative attitude of their pastor. "I think you should go, and I'll pay for the ticket," said one. "I'll go with you!" exclaimed another.

Two weeks afterward, four of us drove into the small mountain town late at night. We were met by the young woman and a friend who led us to the house where we would be staying. When the door was opened, we found ourselves in the middle of a prayer meeting! Brokenhearted but confident of the power of God, people were claiming their friends for Christ. We began to pray with them, and the prayer meeting continued until the early-morning hours.

Even though we sensed that God was working, we were amazed the next evening to find the gymnasium filled with young people and adults. God's power fell on that meeting and swept through the town. During those three days, people from every corner of life, almost 200 of them, confessed Christ as Savior and Lord. Churches were filled the following Sunday; Bible study groups were formed that continued for a great while afterward. It all began when God found an earnest young woman, crying out to Him at a time of need, who was willing to pray through and then act on God's revealed will.

If we decide to enter into the abiding life and consistently seek His will through His Word, we will discover that God is eager to reveal His plan for our behavior. And God always keeps His word!

> *"If My people who are called by My name will humble them-selves, and pray and seek My face, and turn from their wicked ways, then will I hear from heaven, and will forgive their sin and will heal their land."*
>
> — 2 CHRONICLES 7:14

QUESTIONS FOR REFLECTION AND PRAYER

1. Do you find it difficult to acknowledge your need? To ask God for His help? Why? Talk to God about this now.

2. Do you believe God has revealed His will for your life in His Word? Why or why not? Do the Scriptures speak to your life only in general terms or in regard to specific situations and decisions? Explain. Discuss this with God now.

3. Which comes easier in prayer—asking or thanking? Why? Do you usually offer general or specific requests to God? Why? How would you like to improve your prayer life? Ask God to help you with this right now.

4. What specific issue in your life could be resolved if you would find God's will through His Word and pray accordingly? Will you?

8

PRAYER AND
FASTING

*"Is not this the fast
that I have chosen . . . ?"*
ISAIAH 58:6

FOR THE MAJORITY OF BELIEVERS the biblical discipline of fasting is an overlooked element in their practice of prayer. Even though the Bible addresses the topic with exhortation, illustration, counsel, and instruction, many have never seriously considered, much less undertaken, fasting. They associate fasting with the mystic or ascetic; they do not see it as a practice for all Christians.

The role fasting plays in the discipline of prayer is significant, however. Jesus launched his three years of open ministry after forty hidden days and nights of prayer and fasting (Matt. 4:1-11). In His Sermon on the Mount (Matt. 5—7), our Lord gave specific behavioral instructions, including, ". . . *when* you fast" (Matt. 6:16). He clearly saw this as normative for His followers. When the disciples of John the Baptist asked the Lord why His disciples were not fasting, Jesus replied that He would be taken away, ". . . and *then* they will fast" (Matt. 9:15). On one particularly perplexing occasion He told His disciples that deliverance from a certain kind of demonic spirit is possible ". . . by nothing but prayer and fasting" (Mark 9:29).

I do not intend to present here a defense of fasting or instruction in the meaning or methodology of fasting. There is abundant material available on those subjects. But I do want to focus on a major passage that answers the question: What happens when we fast? In Isaiah 58 God associates at least twelve remarkable promises with the practice of fasting. But first He instructs us about improper and proper fasting.

IMPROPER REASONS FOR FASTING

Occasionally a speaker or author will suggest that fasting obligates God to make a specific response. Actually, however, fasting is primarily a means of heart preparation as we bow before Him. Conducted properly, a fast brings increased sensitivity to God, added time for fellowship with Him, and a heightened eagerness to cooperate with Him.

An acquaintance of mine once said, "Things are tough at work. My supervisor is not a Christian. My fellow employees make fun of the church. I'd better fast and get God on their case." His inference was that through fasting he hoped to overcome God's reluctance to make his life more comfortable! This is neither the biblical method nor the correct motivation for fasting.

Israel practiced fasting but often for the wrong reasons. In Isaiah 58 God lists at least four improper reasons for fasting.

Fasting to get God's attention (Isa. 58:3a). "Why have we fasted," they said "and You have not seen? Why have we afflicted our souls, and You've taken no notice?" Israel was frustrated because God's favor and attention had not been aroused by their religious exercise.

Fasting without focusing on the Lord (Isa. 58:3b). "In fact, in the day of your fast you find pleasure, and exploit all your laborers." Fasting had become merely a physical exercise, with no affliction of soul or seeking after God.

Fasting without accompanying humility of heart (Isa. 58:4). "Indeed you fast for strife and debate, and to strike with the fist of wickedness. You will not fast as you do this day, to make your voice heard on high." Fasting is not a way of impressing God with who you are. It is a spiritual discipline that enables you to see His greatness and power more clearly as you humble yourself before Him.

Fasting for a brief external show of piety (Isa. 58:5). "Is it a fast that I have chosen? A day for a man to afflict his soul? Is it to bow down his head like a bulrush, and to spread out sackcloth and ashes? Would you call this a fast, and an acceptable day to the LORD?" God saw that Israel had scheduled a fast for a great outward appearance of spiritual sensitivity. What a show!

Years ago my family and I hired a driver to assist us on our own personal tour of the Holy Land. It was the season during which this man's religion called for fasting. But since his fasting was only required during the day, evenings would find him gorging himself in the restaurants and consuming large amounts of liquor in the bars. The next day our bleary-eyed, irritable driver would roll through the countryside squinting into the sun and struggling to get us to our destination safely. "Why are you fasting?" I asked him. "Oh," he replied, "this is the way I show my devotion to God!" An application of Isaiah 58 would have been appropriate, but Jesus' comments about casting pearls came to mind.

THE PROPER PURPOSES FOR FASTING

In Isaiah 58:6-7 God reveals the appropriate motivations for fasting.

To bring liberation from the bonds of wickedness and to set the oppressed free. Who among us has not come to the conclusion that we seem tied to certain wicked priorities and practices from which we need to be set free? We do not necessarily doubt the overcoming power of God, but for some reason we lack victory in our lives. Fasting prepares our hearts to hear what God has to say on the issues of life so we can take appropriate action and receive the spiritual freedom only He can grant.

To relieve us of heavy burdens. In addition to personal bonds of wickedness, we all carry burdens arising from the everyday stresses and strains of life on this earth. Jesus said, "Come to Me, all you who labor and are heavy laden" (Matt. 11:28). When we fast and listen with our hearts, He will begin sorting through the tangle of our lives and will replace our burdens with His own, which means freedom and peace, "for My yoke is easy and My burden is light" (Matt. 11:30).

To increase our sensitivity toward the needs of others so we can minister to them in a practical manner. "Is it not to share your bread with the hungry, and that you bring to your house the poor who are cast out; when you see the naked, that you cover him . . . ?" (Isa. 58:7). Fasting makes it possible for us to give resources we would otherwise keep for ourselves. When we are not busy feeding our own faces, we can feed others!

To invest ourselves in our families. One who seeks God through fasting will ". . . not hide [himself] from [his] own flesh" (v. 7). Though the discipline of fasting is not for show, it is often good to let family members know of our intent. We will generally find them surprisingly supportive. I have discovered that sitting at a table with my family while I am fasting gives me considerably more time to focus my attention on them, their needs, and their hearts' desires. I am a better listener and a more responsive husband and father because of the clarity of focus produced by fasting.

GOD'S PROMISES TO THOSE WHO FAST FOR HIM

Fasting in harmony with the purposes of God is sure to bring remarkable blessings. In Isaiah 58:8-14 we find God's promised benefits for those who enter this discipline with a serious heart and a spiritual focus.

Insight and understanding. "Then your *light* shall break forth like the morning" (v. 8). The Hebrew word translated "light" here refers to understanding. As we engage in prayer with fasting, God will give us the insight to solve problems and behave with discretion.

The promise of Jeremiah 33:3 is remarkable: "Call to Me, and I will answer you, and show you great and mighty things, *which you do not know.*" God works by His Spirit through His Word to reveal the way He wants us to take.

Remarkable positive changes in physical well-being. "Your healing shall spring forth speedily" (Isa. 58:8). In many instances, fasting for physical purposes alone can have an unusually positive effect on one's health. Coupled with prayer, fasting has brought an unusual sense of well-being to many individuals. These two disciplines can correct both physical and spiritual difficulties, which sometimes have a direct connection.

A deep sense of what is right. "Your righteousness shall go before you" (v. 8). I have a friend to whom I often turn for counsel because he possesses a remarkable ability to go right to the heart of an issue and detect possible violations of scriptural principles. My friend spends a great deal of time each day immersing himself in the Word and in the practice of prayer. He often sets aside time for prayer and fasting as well. I am convinced that the practice of these disciplines has filled him with a sense of righteousness that exceeds his conscious reasoning.

Others' awareness that you have been with God. "The glory of the Lord shall be your rear guard" (v. 8). His majestic presence will follow after us to protect and provide. I call this the unconscious witness of our lives. Without any deliberate effort on our part, others will know we have been with God. This is similar to the radiance of God's glory on the face of Moses. Moses was unaware of this until he was told about it by others.

Some years ago, during a period of sustained fasting, the Lord reminded me of a wrong I needed to correct. I had indicated a desire to purchase an item in an antique store operated by a friend. He had protested, insisting that he be allowed to give it to me. "I will take it," I had said, "but I am going to pay you for it." We both had a good-natured laugh about it. I left with the article, insisting that I would pay him later if he would not take it now. But I never got around to it.

Now God had brought that seemingly insignificant event to my mind. I immediately left the room where I had been praying and fasting and went to the man's business with an apology on my lips and a check in my hand. He was dumbfounded. But this time I was not to be swayed.

Later my friend told me "the rest of the story" with a heart full of joy. "As you turned to leave," he said, "I sensed that you had been with God. I was overwhelmed with the thought of God's power and was moved to do something I had not previously considered possible." He then proceeded to relate how for years he had worn a brace to correct terrible pain in his back. He had that day asked God to bring healing to his back, removed the brace, and now, several days later, was still without pain. He was thanking God for his healing.

I cannot explain that. Nor do I believe it always occurs in this manner. All I know is that the sense that I had been with God somehow moved this brother to pray for healing.

A sense of immediate access to God in your prayer life. "You shall call, and the LORD will answer. You shall cry, and He will say 'Here I am'" (v. 9). Prayer is not meant to pull on the heart-strings of an indifferent Lord. We do not pray to *get* His attention; we pray because we *have* His attention. But the world and our own sin can disrupt our fellowship with God.

Setting aside time to pray and fast brings us face to face with whatever has crept into our lives and is hindering our relationship with God. A missionary to China, Bertha Smith, used to speak about "keeping your sin list short." "Confess them as God convicts you," she would say, " and you can bask in the joy of unbroken fellowship with Him." "If I regard iniquity in my heart, the LORD will not hear" (Ps. 66:18). But "if we confess our sins, He is faithful and just to forgive us our sins and to cleanse us from all unrighteousness" (1 John 1:9).

Release from spiritual oppression. "Your light shall dawn in the darkness, and your darkness shall be as the noonday" (Isa. 58:10). There was a time in my life when I was becoming increasingly cynical of others and simply wanted to be left alone. I was easily provoked and often disgruntled. I felt as if I were living in a dark, suffocating fog.

Since I am by nature an upbeat, optimistic individual, I was perplexed at my inability to pinpoint the problem. Now I realize that I was experiencing spiritual oppression. I was not being strengthened by the joy of the Lord. And I did not know which way to turn.

A friend suggested that I would benefit from a sustained period of prayer and fasting, thus pointing me to both the problem and the cure. I followed his counsel, and suddenly the cloud was lifted, fellowship was restored, and the joy of the Lord returned to my heart.

Moment-by-moment guidance from the Lord. "The Lord will guide you continually" (v. 11). Like the prophet of old, we will hear the Lord saying, "This is the way, walk in it." Every believer should be guided by the principles and counsel of Scripture. But in prayer and fasting a believer finds that sensitivity to divine counsel is especially heightened by an increased awareness of God's presence.

Sailing solo over vast stretches of ocean is undoubtedly a challenging experience, but the principles are the same as when sailing with a full crew. The sails must be trimmed properly, the course must be attended with diligence, and the compass must be followed with extreme caution. The danger comes when the lonely sailor is lulled by a false sense of security and throws caution to the wind as he steers his course.

What comfort there is when another is present to cheer and to guide. Other hands are working; other eyes are watching. Human companions are a comfort, and the fellowship of God even more so. Prayer with fasting brings the believer to a conscious awareness of God's presence, and the Holy Spirit's role as *Paraclete* or "one who comes alongside" is acknowledged with gratitude.

Satisfaction at times and places when and where it would otherwise seem impossible. God will "satisfy your soul in drought" (v. 11; literally, "the scorched places"). Others will marvel that we are finding fulfillment in such an unlikely place, under such unlikely circumstances, and at such an unlikely time. From their vantage point we may seem stuck in a deserted place with none of the amenities or resources they think necessary for fulfillment. Yet this place can truly become *home* to us because the presence of a loving heavenly Father is the controlling reality in our lives.

I am always intrigued by missionary families who are coming to the closing days of their much-needed furlough. Often they express an eagerness to get back "home." In many instances their missionary service occurs under some of the most difficult circumstances imaginable; yet that location has become home to them. There they have seen the hand of God, enjoyed His wonderful presence, and sensed His strength as they put hand and heart to the harvest. God has indeed satisfied their souls during drought.

What about the place of spiritual drought in our lives? God promises that prayer and fasting will make a difference as we discover a restored sense of His presence.

> When earth is hard, and ground is bare
> And all around is dry,
> When flowing water's disappeared
> And no cloud's in the sky.
> Remember this, that deep beneath the soil
> A river's flowing.

And somewhere far across the ridge
A mighty storm is growing.
The day will come, the Lord's ordained,
Though distant it may seem,
When mighty storm gives thirsty ground
A full and flowing stream.

Now, when life is hard and soul is bare,
And your own spirit's dry,
When God's sweet presence's disappeared
And no tear's in your eye,
Remember this, that deep within your heart
A river's flowing.
And somewhere far across the ridge,
A holy storm is growing.
The day will come, the Lord's ordained,
His stream will o'er you roll.
For He's the Shepherd, you're His sheep,
He will restore your soul.

— T. ELLIFF

Increasing strength to accomplish the Lord's work. He will "strengthen your bones" (v. 11). Praying with fasting often results in a surprising renewal of strength so we can accomplish the purposes of God. Those who wait upon the Lord actually experience an exchange of spiritual strength.

Have you not known? Have you not heard? The everlasting God, the LORD, the Creator of the ends of the earth, neither faints nor is weary. His understanding is unsearchable. He gives power to the weak, and to those who have no might He increases strength. Even the youths shall faint and be weary, and the young men shall utterly fall. But those who wait on the LORD shall renew their strength; they shall mount up with wings like eagles, they shall run and not be weary. They shall walk and not faint.

— ISAIAH 40:28-31

To "wait" on the Lord means literally to be "always facing Him." It is not a matter of whiling away time but an attitude of attentiveness and responsiveness to God. Prayer with fasting brings the believer to this position and strengthens the inner man for significant spiritual tasks. The example of Moses, who was called to two extended fasts in a relatively short period of time, is notable. It is also worth remembering that our Lord prayed and fasted for forty days and nights at the very outset of His public ministry.

Fruitfulness through the work of the Holy Spirit within us. "You shall be like a watered garden, and like a spring of water, whose waters do not fail" (Isa. 58:11). Pictured here is a garden with a never-failing artesian spring. Having ever-sufficient water, the garden produces fruit in abundance. The psalmist notes that the man who delights in the law of the Lord and meditates upon it will be like "a tree planted by the *rivers* of water, that brings forth its fruit in its season, whose leaf also shall not wither; and whatever he does shall prosper" (Ps. 1:3).

It has been my experience and the experience of many others that times of prayer and fasting fuel meditation on the Word of God. Several years ago during just such a time in my own life the Lord placed on my heart five specific directions in which I was to challenge the church I was pastoring. To this day I remain impressed with the response of the church and the fruit that continues to be borne as a result.

Recovering and restoring what has been lost by turning away from God. We and like-hearted believers will "build the old waste places; you shall raise up the foundation of many [previous] generations" (Isa. 58:12). Turning away from God has serious consequences. Time is lost, never to be recovered again, and opportunities are forfeited. Yet, in many instances God by His grace restores that which has been lost.

The prophet Joel voiced God's call to "consecrate a fast" (Joel 2:15). His people and their land had been devastated because of their disobedience. God's promise to those who would come to Him with prayer and fasting, with brokenness and repentance was that He would "restore to you the years that the swarming locust has eaten" (Joel 2:25). The important issue was not the fast itself but the brokenness that was to accompany it. If God's people would return to Him with repentant hearts, *then* He would work on their behalf.

Before we let our God-given dreams die on the battlefield of disobedience, we must spend time in prayer with fasting, seeking God's face. Perhaps He will rebuild the wasted places in our hearts and reconstruct our vision on the old foundations as we repent from sin and return to Him.

Gaining a reputation as a rebuilder. "You shall be called the Repairer of the Breach; the Restorer of Streets to Dwell In." God was saying to Israel that though their reputation had been one of disobedience resulting in devastation, all that could change. They could now be known as those who repair, restore, and rebuild.

Some churches, though they may never be known as the fastest growing or most dynamic, have become havens for people whose destroyed lives have been restored by the power of God. These congregations exhibit Christ's Spirit by reaching out to those who seem most helpless and hopeless. I have noticed that the ministers and congregations of these churches are praying people, and their praying is often accompanied by a call to fast. In this way they constantly refocus their priorities and recapture a sense of the heart of Christ.

As we fast for the right reasons, sincerely and wholeheartedly bowing before God, surrendering to whatever He wishes to do in and through us, we will experience these and other promised benefits and will grow in grace and effectiveness of ministry, for the glory of God.

FASTING AND SPIRITUAL REST

Fasting involves a cessation or rest from the fulfillment of normal appetite. Isaiah 58 links fasting to the observation of the Sabbath, the day of rest established by the Lord for His Old Testament people. Israel's disrespect for and desecration of the Sabbath resulted in divine discipline. People who come before God in prayer and fasting develop a renewed appreciation for the holy ordinances of God.

For many believers today, the Lord's day is a time of leisure activities, a day to pursue personal pleasures. Someone may say, "This is the only day of the week I have to myself!" To properly observe the

Sabbath or Lord's day, God requires that "you turn away your foot from the Sabbath, from doing your pleasure on My holy day. And call the Sabbath a delight, the holy of the LORD, honorable, and . . . honor Him, not doing your own ways, nor finding your own pleasure, nor speaking your own words" (v. 13). When we enter into sustained periods of prayer with fasting we will soon acknowledge that unique blessings of rest and peace attend careful obedience to the will of God. These include:

The Lord will become our delight. Believers who focus on the world take pleasure in many things other than the Lord. It is so easy to become enamored with trivial, mindless pursuits that turn our attention away from God. To delight ourselves in the Lord means that we live with Jesus continually on our mind. Our thoughts constantly return to Him. He is thus a refreshing and acknowledged presence in our lives, and He is honored to have our attention.

The Lord will draw us into this kind of relationship as we dwell in His presence. The cessation of our personal activities and the adjustment of our agendas to make time for Him on the Lord's day sets the stage for going deeper with Him. This involves more than just going to Bible study or worship; it is spending the whole day in fellowship with Him.

We will be carried along on the waves of God's movement throughout the earth. "I will cause you to ride on the high hills of the earth," promises the Lord to those who observe the Sabbath (v. 14). Sensitive believers see that God is at work in unique ways all over the world. To coin a popular phrase, our Savior and Lord is making waves. Those who spend time with Him realize the importance of recognizing where He is at work and what He is doing, then joining in with Him. We will guard against trying to do something for God rather than acting in concert with Him, riding the waves of His power and program. We will avoid seeking to generate our own program, then desperately seeking His blessing. Rather, we will seek His will, then cooperate with it.

We will enjoy "the heritage of Jacob" (v. 14). This remarkable statement concludes the Lord's appeal to Israel to approach Him through prayer, fasting, and proper observance of the Sabbath. Jacob's "heritage" was spelled out by the Lord during the patriarch's remarkable vision at Bethel:

> *"I am the LORD God of Abraham your father and the God of Isaac; the land on which you lie I will give to you and your descendants. Also your descendants shall be as the dust of the earth; you shall spread abroad to the west, and the east, to the north, and the south; and in you and in your seed all the families of the earth shall be blessed."*
>
> —GENESIS 28:13-14

It is a matter of historical record that Israel's failure to properly observe the Sabbath resulted in a lengthy period of departure from their land. In Isaiah 58 God was saying that the promise God made to Jacob could be enjoyed only to the extent that they returned to the Lord and His ordinances with their hearts. Then and only then would He bless all the families of the earth through them.

God indicated to Israel that observing the Sabbath properly indicated the condition of their hearts. He is saying no less to us. The spiritual exercises of prayer and fasting help us clearly focus on the importance of establishing scriptural priorities. Then, as we yield ourselves to God to use however He desires, we will bask in His promises and ride the winds of His power!

A FINAL APPEAL

Paul the apostle encouraged the believers in Corinth to run their race with a determination to win. Such a fervent approach to the Christian life requires discipline. "I discipline my body," he wrote, "and bring it into subjection, lest, when I have preached to others, I myself should become disqualified" (1 Cor. 9:27). Paul said that he took extraordinary steps to remind his body that it was not his boss.

Praying with fasting is just such an exercise. It reminds our physical body that there is another more important appetite—a hunger and thirst for God. We ought to regularly consider the promises made to those who properly pray and fast, then, when God calls us to such a discipline, answer without delay.

QUESTIONS FOR REFLECTION AND PRAYER

1. Is prayer with fasting currently a part of your Christian experience? Why or why not? What should be your purpose for prayer and fasting? Discuss this with God now.

2. Which of the benefits God promises will accompany right fasting means the most to you? Why? What do you believe God could accomplish in your life through prayer with fasting? How do you feel about His desire to do this? Why? Talk this over with God right now.

3. Do you need to experience God's rest more consistently or more deeply in your life? Why? Are you being obedient to the Lord in this area? What do you need to do to receive or maintain His rest? What do you need to let God do? Pray about this now.

9

THE PROPER RESPONSE TO
DELAYED ANSWERS

. . . that your prayers
may not be hindered.

1 PETER 3:7

MANY CHRISTIANS HAVE GIVEN UP on the possibility of entering into an effective prayer ministry. They do not doubt that prayer changes things, but they have seen very little, if anything, happen when they pray. Some have turned to prayer during a tragedy, only to suffer crushing disappointment. Others have asked for guidance at critical times but seemed to receive no response from the Lord.

Why are our prayers sometimes unanswered? Are we praying incorrectly? Do we simply fail to recognize the answer when it comes? Is some important quality missing in our life? Have we overlooked some cardinal principle of prayer? Is prayer simply not intended to be an effective ministry for some of us? I have heard individuals offer these and other reasons for a lack of prayer effectiveness.

Prayer is both a privilege and a responsibility for every Christian. Out Lord taught that "men always ought to pray and not lose heart" (Luke 18:1). Since we are commanded to pray, it follows that every Christian can pray effectively.

If our prayer life is faltering, it is probably for one of the following reasons.

BARRIER #1: NEGLECTING PERSONAL HOLINESS

It is important to recognize that we will never sway God by our personal righteousness. Any goodness we possess is found in our relationship to Christ. He is our righteousness. This is the meaning of praying "in Jesus' name." We come to God on the basis of what Christ has done on the cross and through His resurrected life.

Hebrews 4:14-16 reminds us that since "we have a great High Priest who has passed through the heavens, Jesus the Son of God, let us hold fast our confession. For we do not have a High Priest who cannot sympathize with our weaknesses, but was in all points tempted as we are, yet without sin. Let us, therefore, come boldly to the throne of grace, that we may obtain mercy and find grace to help in time of need." Our authority to approach God in prayer is based entirely on the work of Christ. Only because of that are we acceptable to God.

On the other hand, we must remember that persistent sin on the part of the believer prevents effective prayer. "Who may ascend into the hill of the LORD?" asks the psalmist. "Or who may stand in His holy place? He who has clean hands and a pure heart, who has not lifted up his soul to an idol, nor sworn deceitfully" (Ps. 24:3-4). A failure to concentrate on personal holiness shows an arrogant disregard for the work of Christ. Additionally, it gives Satan the opportunity to play out his role as "the accuser of our brethren" (Rev. 12:10).

How often we have undertaken to pray only to be reminded of personal failure in the area of purity. "How can I ask God to deliver me from this crisis?" we lament. "I've been away from Him for such a long time." Tragically, when trouble strikes, we spend much of our time getting ready to pray instead of praying. The guilt from our spiritual failure makes us hesitant to approach our forgiving Father, whereas He is ready and willing to hear the prayer of confession and restore our soul without delay.

Believers are especially prone to sins of presumption—presuming on the love and grace of God and daring to continue in sin despite the Spirit's urging to repent. "God is loving," we reason, "and since I am a Christian, He will forgive me for this sin. Therefore, I will continue in my disobedience for now and will settle accounts with God later on." This rationale is common with Christians who wrestle with habitual sin. Such sin assumes that God is obliged to forgive and will restore intimate fellowship with Him just because we ask. In reality, such a mind-set hardens our heart, making us insensitive to the voice of God. No wonder the psalmist cried, "Keep back Your servant also from presumptuous sins; let them not have dominion over me" (Ps. 19:13).

Jesus insisted that we have not truly repented of any sin that we are still committing. Repentance involves a change of mind with a resulting change of action. How can a believer who is insensitive to something that caused Christ's death expect to be sensitive to the revealed will of God about other matters? "Create in me a clean heart, O God," beseeched David. "Then I will teach transgressors Your ways, and sinners shall be converted to you" (Ps. 51:10, 13). James reminds us, "The effectual, fervent prayer of a *righteous* man avails much" (Jas. 5:16).

BARRIER #2: PRAYING FOR THE WRONG REASONS

Our prayers are sometimes hindered because our motives are impure. "You ask and do not receive," states James, "because you ask amiss, that you may consume it on your pleasures" (Jas. 4:3). In such a case, we pray in order to satisfy a personal desire of the flesh without any regard for God's will or glory. Psalm 37:4 encourages us to "Delight yourself also in the LORD, and He shall give you the desires of your heart." It must be first the Lord, then our heart's desires. If we desire the gift rather than the Giver, we err.

Consider a teenager who has just become old enough to obtain a driver's license. His heart's desire is for an automobile of his own, but he knows his parents must consent to such a purchase. When he approaches them, they cite various indications of his immaturity— poor grades, disrespect for authority, personal sloppiness, a failure to assume responsibilities in the home. They inform him that he must rectify these issues before he can purchase a car.

A remarkable change occurs in the young man's life overnight! His room is clean; he treats his parents with the utmost respect; he has a new neatness in his personal appearance; and wonder of wonders, his grades drastically improve. Impressed with his mature response and thrilled with his attitude toward them, his parents help him buy an automobile.

But then his parents look on with dismay as he immediately slips back into his old habits. His grades go down; his room is a pigpen; he is never home on time; his appearance is unkempt. Obviously he was delighting himself in the promised automobile and *not* in his parents or their desires.

Similarly, we sometimes engage in good behavior hoping to nudge God into giving us what we want. We may even attach exaggerated claims of useful spiritual purpose to that for which we are praying. "Lord, give me this home, and I'll use it to host a Bible study group!" "Lord, if I get that raise, I'll give more money to the church." "Help me get that promotion, and I'll use it to tell more people about You." But God knows our hearts, and He knows whether we are delighting ourselves in Him or merely in the things we want from Him.

Several years ago when my wife and I were discussing Psalm 37:4, I asked her to list the desires of her heart at that time. Since we had just moved into a new home, I asked specifically regarding some furniture we felt we needed. She said we needed a sofa bed so we would have adequate sleeping arrangements for guests. In addition, we desired a large dining table so we could accommodate more people at mealtimes.

We made note of these "desires" and turned our attention to "delight[ing] in the Lord." We even asked Him to change our desires if they were not in accord with His will. On Thursday of the same week, our new neighbors visited us. In the course of conversation, they mentioned a hide-a-bed sofa they had no room for in their home. "Would you be interested in purchasing it?" they asked, not knowing about our prayers. "No," I said since we had no money to make such a purchase. "At least come look at it," he insisted. Imagine my surprise the next day when my neighbor met me at the door saying, "Tom, God told me to give you this sofa." When I protested, he said I should allow him to obey God. That morning we moved the sofa to our home, where it fit beautifully.

At noon the same day, our first guests arrived. Before taking off their coats, they remarked that they had received a substantial Christmas bonus and wanted to purchase something for our new home, preferably a new dining table! In short order, the sofa bed was in the den, the table was in the dining room, and we were delighting ourselves in the Lord and His goodness more and more.

I am not saying we should pray more for things than we do for people. But it is true that if our concerns are the same as God's, if we are truly delighting ourselves in Him, He will answer our prayers.

BARRIER #3: FAILING TO MAINTAIN RIGHT RELATIONSHIPS

Jesus constantly emphasized the importance of being properly related to others—so we can manifest our relationship with Him and so we can have confidence in prayer. Jesus taught His disciples, "And whenever you stand praying, if you have anything against anyone, forgive him, that your Father in heaven may also forgive you your trespasses. But if you do not forgive, neither will your Father in heaven forgive your trespasses" (Mark 11:25-26). Jesus also said, "Therefore if you bring your gift to the altar, and there remember that your brother has something against you, leave your gift there before the altar, and go your way. First be reconciled to your brother, and then come and offer your gift" (Matt. 5:23-24). The Lord tells us to forgive and to seek the forgiveness of others.

It is impossible to have a fruitful prayer life while harboring an unforgiving spirit or adamantly refusing to seek reconciliation with someone we have wronged. God is interested in drawing men into fellowship with Himself. Paradoxically, we often seek the benefits of such fellowship while at the same time abusing our relationships with others whom He also loves. This displeases our Father and makes our prayers ineffective.

Of particular importance is the maintenance of proper relationships with family members. In 1 Peter 3:7, for instance, husbands are exhorted to dwell with their wives "with understanding, giving honor to the wife, as to the weaker vessel, and as being heirs together of the grace of life, *that your prayers may not be hindered.*" When there is a strain in a family relationship, every attempt should be made to effect reconciliation. Family strife hinders the effectiveness of a ministry of intercession. If we cannot pray *with* fellow believers, how can we pray effectively *for* others?

Barrier #4: Looking to the Wrong Supply Source

Christians are notorious for praying to God about a need but trusting in people to answer that need without God's involvement. Sometimes we even tell God who we think is best suited for the job. On other occasions we subtly inform those we think might meet our need that we are "trusting God to answer our prayer."

Though God sometimes answers our prayers through others, *He is our true source of supply.* The apostle Paul exhorted the Christians in Philippi, "Be anxious for nothing, but in everything by prayer and supplication, with thanksgiving, let your requests be made known to God. . . . And my God shall supply all your need according to His riches in glory by Christ Jesus" (Phil. 4:6, 19).

George Müller of Bristol, England, modeled what it means to trust God alone to take care of us. Faced with overwhelming needs as he cared for hundreds of orphans, he remembered Abraham's experience when asked to sacrifice his son—God provided a ram to sacrifice instead of Isaac. Abraham responded by calling the place "The Lord-Will-Provide" (Hebrew, "Jehovah-jireh," Gen. 22:14). Müller determined that he would share the needs of his ministry with God alone, and never with other men. His careful records indicate that God never failed to supply what was needed. Often that supply would be delivered in the most unlikely manner, an evidence that God alone was the source. Though God may not call us to imitate Müller's practice to the letter, He does want us all to understand that He is the fount of every needed blessing, physical or spiritual.

Speaking to other men about our needs before or without speaking to God about them indicates an absence of faith. We often make every attempt to work things out before getting back to the foundation of trusting God and calling upon Him. This truth cannot be overemphasized: *God alone is the Christian's source of supply.* Failure to recognize this key fact will result in hindered prayers.

BARRIER #5: SATAN'S OPPOSITION TO PRAYER

To enjoy effective prayer, we must not only avoid errors that will get in the way of God's answers—we must also remember key spiritual truths concerning prayer. We will consider, for instance, our enemy, who opposes prayer.

We must ever keep in mind that to engage in prayer is to enter the arena of spiritual warfare. We are reminded in Ephesians 6: "we do not wrestle against flesh and blood, but against principalities, against powers, against the rulers of the darkness of this age, against spiritual hosts of wickedness in the heavenly places" (v. 12). For this reason Paul encourages us to "Put on the whole armor of God" (v. 11), "praying always with all prayer and supplication in the Spirit" (v. 18).

The prophet Daniel experienced a delayed answer to prayer because of satanic opposition. After many days of asking God to show mercy to rebellious Israel, he was approached by a heavenly messenger who said, "Do not fear, Daniel, for from the first day that you set your heart to understand, and to humble yourself before your God, *your words were heard*; and I have come because of your words. But the prince of the kingdom of Persia *withstood* me twenty-one days: and behold, Michael, one of the chief princes, came to help me, for I had been left alone there with the kings of Persia" (Dan. 10:12-13). From Daniel's experience we get a glimpse of the warfare that rages between the forces of heaven and hell when a Christian prays.

If we understand the warfare that surrounds our prayers, we will put on the armor of God and exercise our authority by praying (1) in the name of Jesus (i.e., based on our position in Christ); (2) because of the shed blood of Jesus (representing Satan's defeat); and (3) on the basis of God's revealed will (what God has spoken to our hearts through His Word). We must each remember that "He who is in you is greater than he who is in the world" (1 John 4:4).

BARRIER #6: DIVINE PURPOSE

Satan opposes us, but God is for us and is always at work on our behalf, though not always in the way we suppose. In fact, God often deliberately waits to answer our prayers so that His glory and power will be more fully manifested. The eleventh chapter of John tells us Jesus waited so long to respond to the pleas of Mary and Martha for their brother Lazarus that only a miracle of God would suffice. Standing before the tomb of Lazarus, He acknowledged the importance of the moment: "Because of the people who are standing by I said this, so that they may believe that You sent Me" (John 11:42).

Before His ascension Jesus commanded His followers to return to Jerusalem and "wait for the Promise of the Father" (Acts 1:4), praying together in the Upper Room until the Day of Pentecost. At that time Jerusalem would be filled with people from all around the world. God delayed the answer to their prayers until worldwide attention could be drawn to the outpouring of His Spirit.

God promised Abraham and Sarah a son, but many days went by before the fulfillment of that promise. It was only after all self-effort failed and bearing a child was an impossibility that "the LORD did for Sarah as He had spoken. For Sarah conceived and bore Abraham a son in his old age, at the set time of which God had spoken to him" (Gen. 21:1-2).

The Scripture abounds with exhortations to "wait upon the Lord" (Ps. 27:14; Isa. 40:31). Instead of becoming impatient, we should welcome the opportunity to engage in a discipline that will focus attention on the Lord and develop character in our lives. James reminds us that we should "count it all joy when you fall into various trials, knowing that the testing of your faith produces patience. But let patience have its perfect work, that you may be perfect and complete, lacking nothing" (Jas. 1:2-4). Regular, honest conversation with God as we fight the forces of darkness is an essential part of this process.

BARRIER #7: PRAYER THAT LEADS AWAY FROM FAITH

"Commit your way to the LORD," wrote the psalmist. "Trust also in Him, and He shall bring it to pass" (Ps. 37:5). In other words, we are to put our lives in His hands and let Him do the work. Unfortunately, though we often bring our burdens to the Lord in prayer, we sometimes do not leave them there. Apparently, we do not think He is capable of handling them. Rather than truly committing our way to Him, our prayers at times take the form of reminders (as if God had forgotten us) or critical status reports (as if He did not know how things were progressing). It is even possible to pray ourselves out of a position of faith because our prayers are a product of personal anxiety, not of growing confidence in a caring heavenly Father.

Imagine you are facing extremely critical surgery. Fortunately, you are in the best of hospitals and are under the care of a surgeon renowned for his expertise in your area of need. The day before the surgery, your doctor stops by for a visit. "Doctor," you exclaim, "I'm so glad you're on the case. I have total confidence in your ability. I trust you completely and look forward to having my physical ailment fully remedied."

The doctor appreciates your comments and your confidence. A few moments after he leaves, however, you send a nurse scurrying after him. When he returns to your room, you say, "I really mean it! I really do trust you!"

The evening before the surgery, some of your friends drop by for a visit. When you express your relief about having the best possible physician, they mention another surgeon who did a great job on an acquaintance of theirs. After they leave, you quickly phone your doctor. "I really do trust you because I know you're the best. But . . . well, I heard of another skilled doctor, who does the same kind of surgery. Do you know him?"

Later that night you call your doctor again. "My life is going to be in your hands tomorrow. I just wanted to be sure you're aware of that." When he responds in the affirmative, you ask if he has performed this surgery as often as the doctor you mentioned earlier. Since he is not sure, you suggest, "How about having him in the operating room with you, just in case . . ."

Your surgeon, discerning that your confidence is at an all-time low and that your blood pressure is skyrocketing, decides you are in no position to have surgery the next day. Your anxiety has not only replaced your confidence in the doctor but has kept you from receiving needed help.

Rather than praying merely to calm our worried minds, we are to persevere in prayer, recognizing the greatness of the One with whom we are conversing, confident in the ability and desire of our Lord to respond appropriately, willing to accept whatever answer He considers appropriate. We are then to agree with His answer and act upon it.

RESPONDING PROPERLY TO GOD'S DELAYS

There are three main reasons why God sometimes chooses not to answer our prayers: (1) personal sin; (2) satanic opposition; (3) divine purpose. When our prayers are hindered, we should not become discouraged. Instead, we should ask God to show us the reason, then deal with it biblically.

We must acknowledge, confess, and repent of personal sin. First John 1:9 assures us, "If we confess our sins, He is faithful and just to forgive us our sins and to cleanse us from all unrighteousness." What a great promise to any Christian who has allowed sin to obstruct fellowship with the Father.

Since satanic opposition indicates that our prayers are dealing telling blows to the Devil's army, we should not be discouraged by it. Revelation 12:11 gives a critical insight into the Christian's tools for spiritual warfare: "And they overcame him [Satan] by the blood of the Lamb and by the word of their testimony, and they did not love their lives to the death." Using the authority that is ours because of our position in Christ, we must continue to storm the gates of hell and bind "the strong man" (Matt. 12:29).

We should welcome delayed answers to prayer as opportunities to express trust in a sovereign God. We must resist the temptation to take matters into our own hands or to give up. We must submit to God's timing and control if we are to grow stronger in the faith of intercession.

The prophet Jeremiah, facing severe persecution, asked the Lord, in effect, to "hurry up and do something" (Jer. 12:1-4). God's reply indicated that even greater days of testing lay ahead: "If you have run with the footmen, and they have wearied you, then how can you contend with horses? And if in the land of peace, in which you trusted, they wearied you, then how will you do in the floodplains of Jordan?"

(v. 5). The psalmist reminds us to "Rest in the LORD, and wait patiently for Him" (Ps. 37:7).

Since the answer to our prayers rarely comes according to *our* schedule, it is important to respond properly during periods of delay. When our prayers seem to be hindered, we must continually acknowledge the sovereignty of God. Behind the delay is God's determination that we will learn how to pray.

QUESTIONS FOR REFLECTION AND PRAYER

1. In what ways does personal sin interrupt or ruin your prayer life? How does this affect your personal walk, your relationships with your family members and others, your motives for prayer? Pray in detail about this right now.

2. Do you perceive the Devil's opposition in your prayer life? How does the Enemy attack you in this area? What can you do to resist him? Are you taking these measures? Why or why not? Discuss this with God now.

3. How do you generally react to God's delays in answering your prayers? At such times do you trust God or doubt Him? Why? What do you believe to be God's motive for the delays? Talk to Him about this now.

CALLED TO PRAY WITH PASSION

"Listen!

Can you hear the waters

of your Jabbok

off in the distance?

If so, run to your meeting

with the Lord.

It will be the most incredible

prayer experience

of your life. And you will never

be the same again."

10

WHEN YOU FINALLY GET
ALONE WITH GOD

*Then Jacob was left alone; and a Man wrestled
with him until the breaking of day.*

GENESIS 32:24

WE EACH HAVE A JABBOK IN OUR FUTURE. I am not referring to the
literal Middle East stream that bisects the Jordan River as it flows from
the Sea of Galilee to the Dead Sea. The Jabbok to which I am referring
flows on every continent and in every life. Sooner or later each of us,
like Jacob, will meet the Lord there and we can be forever changed.

For some our Jabbok may flow in the breathtaking beauty of a
natural surrounding. But for most of us our Jabbok will flow through
a place of quietness and peace, and there it will mingle with our tears.
Whatever the setting, there is a Jabbok in your future.

Natural ability, diligently applied, can carry an individual to surprising heights in Christian circles. Hard work is so rare these days that
it attracts and impresses others. People who are willing to settle down
and do their job well often have the opportunity to advance into a position of leadership and status.

But God through His grace ultimately brings us face to face with
our inadequacies. *He is determined to deal with spiritual emptiness
whenever and wherever He finds it in our lives.* No matter how hard
we try to hide it, the truth will come out. Like the famed Tower of Pisa,

our seemingly well-ordered and successful lives will begin to lean embarrassingly if they are not properly founded.

Jacob's life is a perfect illustration of this truth. By cleverness he obtained his brother's birthright. In deceptive partnership with his mother he stole his brother's blessing. Then, running for his life, he spent a night at Bethel and vowed to God that he would not forget Him. He promised that one day he would return home and there erect an altar to God.

But what goes around comes around. At first it appeared that Jacob had met his match in the person of his surreptitious father-in-law. But again Jacob applied himself diligently and begged God for His blessing. God answered graciously, and Jacob began to prosper in cattle, wealth, and children. Jacob was a man with exceptional talent, a brilliant mind, a strong back, and a God-blessed future.

At the height of his glory, frustrated by his father-in-law, Jacob returned to his homeland. But instead of receiving a glorious welcome, he learned that his brother had gathered a small army and was seeking his life. Once again Jacob went to the well of his quick-wittedness that had so often been his ally. He sent flocks and herds of animals to appease his materialistic brother. He divided his extended family and their servants into two groups and sent them separate ways for their safety. Then in a final act of desperation he sent his remaining family members across the Jabbok. Exhausted, he slumped to the ground with the realization that he had reached into the bag of his own human ability and had pulled out his last trick.

Now under the silent stars a most unusual scene transpires: Jacob wrestles with a man. Through the night the patriarch struggles, with no success. He cannot rid himself of his adversary. Who is this man who has come against him?

The answer come in a surprising fashion. As they wrestle, the man brushes the hollow of Jacob's thigh with such might that his hip socket becomes dislocated. In awe at his opponent's incredible strength and power, reflecting on this most unusual battle, Jacob suddenly understands: the One against whom he has been wrestling all night is none other than the Lord Himself!

The wrestling match is a telling picture of Jacob's life. He has sought to achieve success with his cleverness and determination. "Supplanter," the meaning of "Jacob," was an appropriate name for one so driven by ambition. Suddenly seeing his own mortal shortcomings and how much he needed God's help, Jacob clings to the Lord and humbly but persistently asks for a blessing.

Waiting's not the life that I would choose
For, if I wait, I'm confident that I would surely lose
The things I've dreamed about and hoped for and desired
The thrill of saying, "These are things I have acquired!"

No, waiting's not the life that's meant for me.
While others wait I'll move ahead and shortly they will see
The kind of man I am, my cleverness, my drive
Pursuing all my greatest dreams while still alive.

For waiting seems to be a waste of time.
How can the man who stops and waits
achieve those heights sublime
From which to view the lives of those who slowly plod
And only wish to see the places I'll have trod?

Ah, waiting is a sickness, don't you see?
Afflicting young and old alike, but not the likes of me
. . . except that, lately, every way I've turned is closed.
Perhaps the secret's not in pushing on as I'd supposed.

So what's the answer for my struggling soul?
I must confess I've just now seen it in the Book of old
Which says that all the gains and victories I've scored
Are empty, unless first I've waited on the Lord.

For those who wait on Him will find, at length,
An even greater vision and a sure supply of strength.
A mounting up to heights where only eagles soared
Is promised to us if, first, we wait upon the Lord.

— T. Elliff

Jacob's life was never the same after that meeting with the Lord at Jabbok. Admitting his need and inadequacy, he prayed to God with desperation and persistence, and God granted His request with abundance. From that moment on Jacob began to realize the full significance of doing God's work God's way with God's power.

Every believer's life is marked by significant turning points, special meetings with God ordained to bring about radical change. Does your heart long for such meetings with the Lord? Have you come to the point where you know it is futile to press on without Him? There is a Jabbok in your future, and at the heart of such an experience is an honest, help-me-or-I'll-die prayer.

MEETING GOD: OUR CIRCUMSTANCES

Do any of the following describe us? If so, God is calling us to meet with Him.

Desperation

Jacob knew he was facing issues too big for him to handle. He recognized that he might lose everything—his family, his fortune, his future in the place where he had longed to spend the balance of his years. He stood to lose all that made his life worthwhile.

Is God is calling us to Himself through desperate circumstances? Have we been forced against a wall of human weakness? Have we reached into the bag of our own cleverness and found it empty? Have we come to the point where it is difficult to make ourselves keep pushing on? This kind of desperation sometimes prepares us to meet with the Lord.

Destitution

Jacob was not without material resources at that moment. But he had exhausted the depths of his perseverance. I remember visiting with a man who confessed to being "spiritually broke." When I asked what he meant, he replied, "I have always been able to come up with some new idea to add excitement and the appearance of success to my life. Some new project would absorb my energy and attention. It always had to be something big, something great, something life-changing that would capture the attention and admiration of others. I was always looking for something that had in it the promise of greatness and notoriety."

He continued, "Lately nothing has created the slightest bit of interest in my heart. I have become aware that I am great with men but not with God. I have money in my pocket, but I'm spiritually broke!" God was calling him to his own Jabbok.

Dread

Fear obviously filled Jacob's heart. His actions demonstrated utter panic. A wrong turn at that moment would mean destruction. He might never see his family again. His fortune could be lost. All he had worked so hard to accumulate could be gone in a moment, a consequence of his own wrong decisions and actions years earlier. He did not want to think about his past, but he was even more afraid to consider his future (at least if Esau had anything to do with it).

I am acquainted with people (and so are you) who dread making any major decision because they fear they will make the wrong one. They feel as if any moment they might lose their family, their work, their ministry, or their faith. When you speak to them about the bright prospects of the future, they grimace. With pursed lips, a furrowed brow, and a pensive look, they inform you that things are not looking so well for them. For them, the day is never partly sunny but always partly cloudy; their cup is always half-empty, never half-full. These folks, paralyzed by fear, need to meet with the Lord.

Demand

Jacob was under pressure to decide what he should do. The clock was ticking. This was no time to tread water or run in place. His brother was dangerously close, and Jacob did not have another night, much less another day, to make his decision.

At deadline moments decisions must be made. Our failure to decide gives others the power to decide for us, sometimes with disastrous results. People in this situation often complain, "My life is out of control! I have no time of my own! My frantic pace scarcely gives me time to breathe!" In such a dilemma there is no time to waste. We must meet with God!

Interestingly, Jabbok meetings with the Lord often occur in the more mature stages of our spiritual pilgrimage, when the stakes are often the highest, there is more to lose, the pressure is greatest, and recovery from the devastating effects of an earlier wrong decision seems least likely. It is then that the rippling waters of Jabbok are heard most clearly and sought most desperately. God always hears and answers the honest prayers of those in such straits.

MEETING GOD: OUR CONDUCT

Over the years I have developed an appreciation for the biographies of great Christians. Inevitably as I begin reading, I ask myself, "What is this person's secret?" I want to know what distinguishes this individual's walk with God from that of others. Often I am surprised with just how much these individuals have in common, especially in their special meetings with God. Their Jabboks are quite similar to Jacob's. Three characteristics particularly stand out.

Resistance

"Then Jacob was left alone; and a Man wrestled with him until the breaking of day" (Gen. 32:24). Jacob resisted the control of his opponent, doing all he could to insure that the man with whom he wrestled did not gain mastery over him. If only Jacob had known the true identity of the One he considered his adversary!

Our meetings with the Lord generally begin with similar resistance. Though in our minds we understand that the Lord knows best, in our heart we rebel against His control. Wanting things our way, we are determined to prove that we are capable of managing our own lives.

The Lord could literally have crushed Jacob at any moment. But He is not interested in mastering our lives by force. Occasionally, as in the case of Jacob, He will brush against our lives in such a way that we sense the magnitude of His power. But He does not manipulate us into allegiance.

God desires our willing surrender! Have we given everything to

Him? This surrender involves ambitions, position, family, friends—everything! Our first response is often resistance, but He deserves all that we are and have. "I beseech you therefore, brethren, by the mercies of God, that you present your bodies [that is, your entire selves] a living sacrifice, holy, acceptable to God, which is your reasonable service" (Rom. 12:1).

Revelation

"And when He [the Lord] saw that He did not prevail against him [Jacob], He touched the socket of his hip; and the socket of Jacob's hip was out of joint as He wrestled with him" (Gen. 32:25). In this momentary brush with the power of the Lord, Jacob suddenly understood whom he was resisting, and at that point the struggle assumed a totally different nature. Having seen God (undoubtedly the preincarnate Christ), Jacob was remarkably changed and had no desire to let Him go. And his life turned a corner because of this encounter!

Our Lord promised that "the pure in heart" will "see God" (Matt. 5:8). In our spiritual struggles it is often only when we come to a position of urgent abandonment that we "see" the Lord. A friend of mine once stated that desperation generally precedes revelation. Jacob would agree!

Request

When Jacob understood that his fellow wrestler was the Lord, he realized what utter folly it was to resist Him. He also refused to allow the meeting to pass without making two specific requests.

First, *he sought the blessing of the Lord*. "I will not let You go unless You bless me" (Gen. 32:26). As we saw earlier, God's blessing is a sovereign act by which He causes someone or something to supernaturally produce more than is naturally possible. How deeply do we want God to bless us? How hungry are we for His working within us and through us? Is this a matter of casual prayer or earnest entreaty?

Many Bible passages encourage us to pray with perseverance, to "pray and not lose heart" (Luke 18:1). We sometimes get discouraged and stop praying when God's answer does not come quickly enough. Instead, we should persist and hang on until God blesses us. We need more men and women of God who, like Epaphras, are "always wrestling in prayer" (Col. 4:12), determined to keep praying unless God directs us to stop or pray differently.

Jacob also had a second request: *"Tell me Your name*, I pray" (Gen. 32:29). In Old and New Testament times, an individual's name stood for all that he was as a person. Jacob was saying, "I want to know who You are and what You are like—I want to know You!" Having the blessing of God on your life is one thing; knowing God is another.

Similarly, when Moses pled for Israel on Mount Sinai, his request was for more than protection, direction, or sustenance. "If Your presence does not go with us, do not bring us up from here. For how then will it be known that your people and I have found grace in Your sight, except You go with us?" (Exod. 33:13). Moses considered knowing the Lord to be absolutely essential.

Paul echoed this emphasis when he declared that his life's magnificent obsession was to "know" Christ (Phil. 3:10). Similarly, as a result of Jabbok, Jacob's great desire was to enjoy a walk of unhindered fellowship with the Lord. When we have our own Jabbok, every other desire will seem insignificant in our quest to know Him.

MEETING GOD: THE CONSEQUENCES

Some years ago I heard a seminary professor remark, "A person may be religious and lost, but he cannot meet Christ without being changed." Anyone who has an encounter with the Lord, at whatever stage of his spiritual pilgrimage, will be genuinely changed in several specific ways.

A New Description

Jacob was given a new name as a result of meeting the Lord. "Your name shall no longer be called Jacob, but Israel; for you have struggled with God and with men, and have prevailed" (Gen. 32:28). Just as the different names of God reveal different aspects of His personality, so Jacob's new name revealed something about his new nature. As Abram had become Abraham, and as Saul the persecutor would become Paul the apostle, so Jacob the supplanter became Israel the prince.

When we meet with God, our lives will manifest a difference. A drunkard, implicated in the killing of a man in a barroom brawl, was punished by having the dead man's initials, G.M., tattooed on his forehead. In later years he was converted to Christ and subsequently became characterized by a humble life of total surrender to God. One day two young boys were discussing the meaning of the initials on his forehead. "I'm not sure what they mean," said one of the boys, "but my daddy says he thinks they stand for God's Man!"

You may be discouraged about how you are seen by others these days. Perhaps you have been misunderstood because of past or present events over which you had or have no control. Or perhaps your reputation was sullied by deliberate sin and failure. No matter! Go to Jabbok, meet with the Lord, and as you pray to and commune with Him, He will impress upon your life a new name.

A New Direction

Jacob now began to carry out God's will for his life in a new way. That God had a plan for him had never been in question. God had revealed that fact to his parents, and Jacob had sensed it in the earliest years of his development. But how was Jacob to carry out that plan? Until Jabbok, he had sought to achieve God's favor and blessing through his own skill and cleverness. He was determined not to be denied anything he desired. But now, as Israel, he saw that *God's plan must be accomplished by God's power.*

Our meeting with God can be as transforming as Jacob's. Perhaps, like Jacob, we have never doubted that God has a wonderful plan for our lives. Maybe we have even sought to cooperate with Him in achieving the goals we have set. We may have agreed with Him on the crucial issues of our lives. But somewhere along the way we began to depend on our own cleverness and drive. Bold, passionate prayer in a direct encounter with God can change everything! At our Jabbok we can receive God's direction and enabling, then forge forward with His power!

A New Devotion

From that time on, Jacob viewed God differently than before. In fact, Jacob named the place where he wrestled with the Lord Peniel, "For

I have seen God face to face, and my life is preserved" (Gen. 32:30). He now realized that the Lord held sway over life and death and over every corner of his existence and service.

Jacob did not become perfect at Jabbok. Even after that remarkable encounter, he sometimes acted more like a Jacob, at other times more like an Israel. (Simon Peter had a similar experience.) But there was clearly a new devotion in Jacob's life as evidenced by the erection of an altar to the God of Israel.

It must also be noted that Jacob's new identity, direction, and devotion did *not* release him from all the consequences of his past activities. His sons, for instance, had seen too much of the old Jacob. Once back in Canaan, they gave themselves to so much sin that God had to take them (and their descendants) to Egypt for a 400-year period of discipline and training. Nevertheless, God honored Jacob's devotion and fulfilled His plan through his children.

A certain quiet holiness characterizes the lives of those who have been to the Jabbok. They have erected altars in their hearts. To visit with them is to be drawn into an experience of worship. They walk on holy ground. They have a renewed devotion to the gracious God they serve.

A New Distinction

Jacob bore a physical reminder of his meeting with the Lord: "Just as he crossed over Penuel, the sun rose on him, and he limped on his leg" (Gen. 32:31). Jacob was marked by his meeting with the Lord. His lame limb became to him what Paul's "marks of the Lord Jesus" (Gal. 6:17) were to him—reminders of God's ownership.

People who have met the Lord and surrendered to Him are marked for life. A seminary student once told me that following his conversion he had a hard time forgetting the dirty jokes he loved to tell before getting saved. But he went on to explain, "I find it difficult to repeat those jokes to others now, even though I can remember them." Later on, after a Jabbok experience with the Lord, he reported, "You know, the strangest thing has happened. There was a time when I could remember certain jokes but felt ashamed to tell them. Now I find it difficult, impossible in fact, even to remember them." Meeting the Lord and surrendering to Him makes a radical difference in a man's life. It is a turning point without equal.

In Conclusion

Before he died, Jacob came face to face once again with his son Joseph, whom he thought had been killed. This time the reunion occurred, not in Canaan, but in Egypt where Joseph had risen to power. There Jacob's entire family enjoyed Egypt's provisions during a time of severe famine.

Picture Jacob as an old man, with grandchildren and great-grandchildren gathered around him as he limps over to a chair or couch. "Tell us the story," the children beg him, "about the wrestling match that made your leg the way it is." Settling himself comfortably, Jacob says, "Well, this happened because I wrestled with the Lord. You see . . ."

Listen! Can you hear the waters of your Jabbok off in the distance? If so, then run to your meeting with the Lord! It will be the most incredible prayer experience of your life! And you will never be the same again!

Questions for Reflection and Prayer

1. Are you facing any circumstances now that cause you to feel desperate or bankrupt or terrified? Are you willing to persevere in prayer about them, or are you determined to work things out through your own cleverness or ambition? Why? Talk this over with God right now.

2. Is God initiating or continuing a personal encounter with you these days? Are you welcoming or resisting this? Why? Are you willing to let God reveal more of Himself to you and to request His help? Why or why not? Pray about all this now.

3. Have you had a Jabbok experience that brought a new identification, new direction, new devotion, or a new appreciation of Christ's lordship? With what results? What should happen next? Discuss these matters with God now.

11

PRAYING FOR
ANOTHER PERSON

"So now I will go up to the LORD.*"*

EXODUS 32:30

AS A PASTOR I RECEIVE many requests to pray for specific individuals. In each case I seek to respond as conscientiously as possible, often
praying with the person making the plea before our conversation ends.
I count this a high privilege, especially when I hear later about how the
prayer was answered. On some occasions, however, God urges me to
go a step further—to be an intercessor for another person. We will
examine the difference in this chapter.

Several years ago I received an urgent call from the distressed
father of a newborn. "Pray for my son!" he requested. "The doctors
have discovered a serious difficulty and say he might die in the next
few hours." I assured him of my prayers and told him I would meet
him at the hospital in a matter of minutes.

As I was preparing to leave for the hospital, God burdened my
heart with the critical needs of that baby. I slipped to my knees beside
my bed and began to pray. I also examined the Scripture passage I had
been reading when the young father called. God assured me by His
Spirit through His Word that the child would not only survive this crisis but would live to become a great witness for God. Thanking the
Lord for His promise, I drove to the hospital, where the exuberant parents had just received word from the doctors that the child had

responded to treatment and would most surely be well enough to go home in a few days.

It is always a challenge when we discover God has chosen us to play an integral part in the lives of others through the practice of intercessory prayer. Why God chose to reveal His will in a matter of minutes but on other occasions does not do so for months or even years, I do not know. But Scripture does tell us that before God performs a great ministry, He generally reveals the nature of that ministry to someone who is praying.

THE MEANING OF INTERCESSION

There is a difference between simply praying for people and true intercession. While all intercession involves prayer, all praying for others is not necessarily intercessory. The apostle Paul referred to this distinction when he wrote, "Therefore I exhort first of all that supplications, *prayers*, *intercessions*, and giving of thanks be made for all men" (1 Tim. 2:1). Intercession is, by nature, the exercise by which an individual positions himself between two parties—one with a need and the other with the answer—and seeks to bring the two together. It is a matter of reaching out to take the hand of the one with the problem and reaching up to take the hand of the One with the provision and being willing to sacrifice whatever is necessary so that they meet.

James 4:17 reminds us that "to him who knows to do good and does not do it, to him it is sin." Since prayer is not an option for the Christian but is commanded by God, it is a sin *not* to pray. Realizing this and desiring to have a positive spiritual impact on the lives of friends and loved ones, many Christians want to have a ministry of intercession but are not certain how to begin or develop it. Fortunately, God has given us a biblical pattern for intercession from the life of Moses.

You probably remember that while Moses was on Sinai receiving the commandments of God, a tragic event was taking place in the camp below. Assuming Moses would never return, the Israelites encouraged Aaron to make a golden calf so they could worship it.

When Moses did in fact return to the camp, they were worshiping with drunken revelry and idolatry.

After breaking the tablets of the law at the base of Mount Sinai, Moses turned his attention to the sin of Israel. He ground the golden calf into powder, poured it into some water, and made the Israelites drink it. (This is an excellent example of the way God can turn the object of our sinful delight into the object of our discipline, for our correction and His glory.) Moses gathered around him the sons of Levi, men who were unashamedly on the Lord's side. They then began to slay with the sword the ungodly Israelites, killing almost 3,000 people. Unquestionably, God's wrath was being poured out that day.

The next day Moses again ascended Mount Sinai to intercede for the people. Notice the pattern of intercession the patriarch followed when Israel's future was hanging in the balance. It is the same to be followed by anyone desiring to intercede for another.

THE PURPOSE OF INTERCESSION

In intercession we seek the grace of God for an individual or individuals, so that fellowship with God and usefulness for Him will be established or maintained. The major focus of the intercessor is finding and cooperating with God's will.

"You have committed a great sin," Moses said to the children of Israel. "So now I will go up to the LORD; perhaps I can make atonement for your sin" (Exod. 32:30). Moses assumed the position of an intercessor ("I will go up to the LORD") for a specific purpose (expressed by the word "atonement," which here refers to an act of grace by which offenses were covered so fellowship could be restored between the offender and the one offended). In other words, Moses pled with God to cover the sins of Israel so fellowship between God and His people could be reinstated. Such an act would be based entirely upon God's merciful gift of forgiveness.

Believers sometimes say, "I'm praying for a certain person to receive physical healing," or "I'm praying for someone who desperately needs a job." Such prayers may express the desires of our hearts. But what does God want for that individual? What does He see as necessary to bring that person to salvation or back into fellowship with Himself so that he might grow in grace or to become a more effective servant of Christ? Are we ourselves willing to wait before Him and to align ourselves with His revealed will?

I have heard sincere Christians say to someone undergoing a trial, "I have prayed that God will work this out in a certain way, and I just know He's going to do it." Too often they do not really "know" but only "hope." They may be trying to push God into handling the situation their way by putting His reputation at stake. But all they accomplish is to delay the individual's coming into conformity with God's will.

Consider, for instance, the loving mother who prays, "Lord, bring my son home; don't let him suffer harm." It may indeed be God's will for him to return home. It may also be true that apart from experiencing harm, he will return the same as when he left, having missed out on the growth that comes only through affliction. This is not to say that we should throw up our hands in resignation to sickness, heartache, or other tragic situations. But the point is, *the basic purpose of intercession is fellowship with God through His mercy and grace, through whatever means or circumstances He deems best.*

Notice that Moses made no promises, raised no false hopes, and did not give any unfounded assurances. "You have committed a great sin . . . perhaps I can make atonement for your sin." He realized that apart from God's grace, the children of Israel could no longer enjoy the presence of God. As he climbed Sinai to make intercession before the Lord, he had that specific purpose in mind.

HONESTY BEFORE GOD

Have you ever noticed that often we do not tell the One who knows our hearts what is really in our hearts? We sometimes attempt instead to impress God with the credentials of the person for whom we are praying. Consider the mother praying for her wayward son: "Lord, You know my son is a good boy." If she were honest she might admit that her son is wicked and deserves God's chastening. (And, of course, even the best of us are self-willed sinners apart from God's grace.)

In contrast, "Moses returned to the LORD and said, 'Oh, these people have committed a great sin, and have made themselves a god of gold'" (Exod. 32:31). Moses admitted both the wickedness of Israel and the specific manner in which their sinfulness was manifested. *True intercession faces the facts*—no facade, no denial, but rather agreement with God's assessment of the situation. Moses did not say, "Lord, these folks have been through so much. You know they're good at heart. Given a second chance, they'll do better. They're just tired or stressed out, that's all." He said instead, "These people have committed a great sin."

How should we pray for our friend who may be experiencing a grave physical illness? First, acknowledge the problem as specifically as possible, then request sufficient grace to enable the individual to maintain a close and useful fellowship with God. And we must be willing to be part of God's answer if He so chooses. If our friend's affliction is a result of personal sin, we must ask God by His grace to bring him or her to an undeniable recognition of the sin, followed by confession and repentance.

On the eve of His crucifixion Jesus was moved to intercede not only for His disciples, "but also for those who will believe in Me through their [the disciples'] word; that they all may be one, as You, Father, are in Me, and I in You; that they also may be one in Us, that the world may believe that You sent Me" (John 17:20-21). Notice that the two basic issues of Jesus' intercession were *fellowship* ("that they also may be one in Us") and *usefulness* ("that the world may believe").

Intercession is more than praying in general terms for a person. Neither is it an attempt to play on God's sympathy. *Intercessors seek the mind of God.* Therefore, it is crucial that we identify exactly what is at stake. We must not overlook the importance of stating the problem in as specific terms as possible.

THE PASSION OF INTERCESSION

A true intercessor identifies with the person for whom he is praying and is willing to go to any length to secure God's grace for that individual. This is why so few Christians enter into the labor of intercession. It is the most demanding—and the most fruitful—ministry we can have!

Listen to Moses' passionate prayer for his people: "Yet now, if You will forgive their sin—but if not, I pray, blot me out of Your book which You have written" (Exod. 32:32). Having addressed the problem, Moses made a specific plea: "forgive their sin." Notice several things about the manner in which Moses presented his plea.

Moses was still seeking the mind of God. "If You will . . ." He did not yet know God's will regarding the future of Israel. Faith springs from truth revealed by God, and Moses was awaiting God's final word on the situation. Intercessors recognize that God's timing may not be theirs and that they need to persevere in prayer for others.

Moses was asking God to deal with the problem, not the symptom. "If you will forgive their sin . . ." Their problem was *sin*, which was manifested by their making a god of gold. True intercession must deal with root causes rather than symptoms. A man with tuberculosis may have a serious cough, but if his physician treats only the cough, he is not dealing with the real problem and is in fact endangering his patient's life. In the same way, if we soothe people's hurts but do not ask God to help us see beneath the surface, we cannot intercede effectively. We must, as far as possible, see the specific issues involved and trust the Holy Spirit to make up for our limited understanding (see Rom. 8:26-27).

Moses identified with the people for whom he was interceding, positioning himself between God and them. "But if not, I pray, blot me out of Your book which you have written." It is interesting that Moses knew at least something about God's "Book of Life" (Rev. 21:27). But of greater significance is the fact that Moses was dead serious about his intercession, so much so that he staked his life on the outcome. And he would intercede until God gave him an answer.

Jesus is the supreme example of positioning oneself between God and the individual being prayed for, no matter what the cost. He "made Himself of no reputation, taking the form of a bondservant, and coming in the likeness of men. And being found in fashion as a man, He humbled Himself and became obedient to the point of death, even the death of the cross" (Phil. 2:7-8). This is why the Crucifixion is often identified as Christ's "Passion."

PRAYER AND PROMISE

Apparently the intercession of Moses for the children of Israel lasted many days. At one point God agreed to allow Moses to lead the Israelites to Canaan, promising protection and direction. But God said, "I will not go up in your midst" (Exod. 33:3). Realizing that Israel could not survive without the presence of God, Moses *continued* to intercede. A tabernacle for intercession stood outside the camp for "everyone who sought the LORD" (v. 7), and there Moses and the Lord talked "face to face, as a man speaks to his friend" (v. 11).

It was during one of these times that Moses called to mind what God had already promised concerning the welfare of Israel (v. 12). He then pled that the presence of God would be restored: "For how then will it be known that Your people and I have found grace in your sight, except You go with us? So shall we be separate, Your people and I, from all the people who are upon the face of the earth" (v. 16).

Moses requested an act of grace that would allow fellowship *with* God and usefulness *for* God, and the Lord finally responded with this promise: "I will also do this thing that you have spoken; for you have found *grace* in My sight, and I know you by name" (v. 17). Just as Abraham had interceded successfully for backslidden Lot, so Moses had interceded for Israel and secured the promise of God for his people. Oh, the power in passionate, interceding prayer!

A FINAL ILLUSTRATION

During a prayer time several years ago I listened as a grief-stricken father shared the burdens of his heart. His daughter had left home after a continuing series of family conflicts. Several days of searching had failed to locate her, and her parents had discovered evidence that her rebellious attitude had brought her into the company of the most questionable individuals.

Fortunately for both the girl and her family, her parents knew how to employ biblical intercession. After weeks of prayer and searching in the Word, the father shared that God had given him a Bible promise regarding the welfare of his daughter and indeed his entire family: "Your wife shall be like a fruitful vine in the very heart of your house, your children like olive plants all around your table. Behold, thus shall the man be blessed who fears the LORD" (Ps. 128:3-4).

As is so often the case, the situation seemed to worsen almost immediately. There was virtually no communication with the daughter, and the pressures associated with her absence created additional problems for the family. But the faithful parents kept praying according to God's revealed will.

After almost a year I received a telephone call from the daughter requesting a conference. Although she had wanted to avoid meeting her parents, the Lord ordained a providential reunion in the church parking lot before she entered the building. Imagine my surprise to find all three of them waiting at my office door. During the moments that followed, I heard a firsthand testimony to the effectiveness of intercession.

The young lady told us that months earlier she had married, only to witness her husband's being arrested shortly afterward on a drug charge. While in jail he had been introduced to Christ and was born into the family of God. Calling his young wife to the jail, he told her how he had come into personal relationship with Christ, led her to make a similar commitment, and encouraged her to locate her parents so they could both ask forgiveness. She had requested the conference to ask how best to go about reestablishing a relationship with her parents. But by the time of the conference, it was all already settled!

Over the next few months the parents visited their son-in-law on a regular basis, assured him of their support, and encouraged him in Christian growth. Since then he has been released from prison, and both he and his wife are actively serving the Lord. Both parents have had the thrill of seeing their entire family assembled "like olive plants all around your table."

God is eager to make a covenant with those who are willing to enter into the ministry of intercession. We can, like Moses, like those parents, reach up to take the hand of God, reach out to take the hand of man, and bring the two together.

QUESTIONS FOR REFLECTION AND PRAYER

1. How are prayer in general and intercession in particular different? Have you personally been or are you now an intercessor? Why or why not? Do you desire increased effectiveness in this area? Talk to God about this now.

2. What is the true purpose of intercession? What kinds of thinking can thwart this? Do you find it easy or hard to be honest with God about those for whom you are interceding? Why? Discuss this with God now.

3. In what ways can you identify with those for whom you want to be an intercessor? Are you willing to be part of the answer? What price are you willing to pay to see God do His work in the other person's life? Pray regarding this right now.

12

PRAYING FOR THE GRACE TO FORGIVE

"So My heavenly Father also will do to you
if each of you, from his heart, does not forgive
his brother his trespasses."

MATTHEW 18:35

HAVE YOU EVER WONDERED how much of your present behavior is a reaction to bitter experiences in your past? I have talked with individuals whose obsession with clothing stemmed from an embarrassing comment made by a grade school friend. I know of marriages that have crumbled because of hurtful circumstances and the laceration of soul that accompanied them. I have met ministers who have been crowded into dark corners of uselessness because they are unwilling to deal properly with wounds inflicted by some church, committee, or individual. A missionary once confessed that he was perhaps serving overseas merely to disprove the criticisms of a lady who told him, "You don't care about missions at all!"

The manner in which we deal with hurtful events from our past affects us physically and emotionally. Even if separated by years and miles, that rejection, that scalding of emotions, that wounding of heart can render us useless and bitter if we fail to deal with it in a scriptural manner. Difficult circumstances of yesteryear or yesterday can cause our adrenaline to flow, our pulse rate to climb, our food to taste bitter. On sleepless nights they can cause our mind to reel with what others have said or done to us and what we should have done or said in response.

AN INESCAPABLE CHOICE

Bitter experiences of the past also affect us spiritually. If we refuse to forgive, we will find our fellowship with God disrupted and our prayers rendered powerless. That is why our Lord spoke so often and so passionately about forgiveness.

At some point in our lives each of us must deal with the issue of forgiveness. But what does it mean to forgive? If you have said, "I forgive, but I cannot forget," have you forgiven at all? Are some offenses so terrible that God will excuse your inability or refusal to forgive? Will forgiving an offender send a wrong signal, somehow indicating not only acceptance but approval of the offense? What do these matters have to do with our relationship with God, and our prayer life in particular?

Each of us is aware that the Lord has commanded us to forgive. But how are we to do it? Is forgiving simply a mind game, intellectual gymnastics? Or is there some way to genuinely wash our souls of hurt and release ourselves and the other person from the offense and its effects? Is there some way we can stop reacting angrily and start cooperating with God's design for our lives, receiving and passing on His forgiveness?

Several years ago God showed me my deficiency in the area of forgiveness. Since He calls His children to be conformed to the image of Christ, He set a program in motion to deal with that shortcoming in my life. Today He is still teaching me about forgiveness. Class is still in session; the pilgrimage is not over! But here is my story.

Some years ago, not long after my family and I went to Africa, my wife and children were involved in a very serious accident, leaving my eldest daughter critically injured. Lying in a hospital, she was for a time at the very point of death. The third day following the accident, I received a phone call from a police officer in a town not far from where the accident occurred. He asked me to come to his office so we could discuss some matters regarding the incident.

I assumed that the purpose of our discussion was to inform me that since it was a single vehicle accident, my wife was going to be charged with negligence. Instead he said, "We believe the accident occurred because someone tampered with your vehicle." He then proceeded to show me photographs and other evidence to support his conclusion. He believed that the accident was caused by individuals wanting to steal the vehicle. We agreed that a search for the guilty parties would be fruitless.

That evening as I traveled back to our hometown, I felt anger boiling in my heart. I wanted to scream out to God, "Where were You when we needed You?" Upon arriving at our house, I fell on my knees and said, "Dear God, I came to this country to minister to these people, but I feel so angry. You are going to have to teach me how to forgive." God answered that prayer, and during the following weeks He led me to Jesus' parable in Matthew 18:23-35.

BEING FORGIVEN—FORGIVING

Jesus told of a certain king whose servant owed him an enormous sum. His debt, in fact, would have been absolutely unpayable had he lived several lifetimes. Angry over the unpaid debt, the king commanded that the debtor's children and wife be sold and the man himself put into prison until the debt was paid. The man prostrated himself before the king, begging him to give him more time to pay what he owed.

Remarkably, the king responded with compassion. With a heart of mercy (perhaps knowing he did not need the money anyway), the king did more than grant the man a few more days—he forgave him for the entire debt! But sadly, this same servant went out, found a fellow servant who owed him a small amount—pocket change!—grabbed the servant by the neck, shook him, and said, "Give me what you owe me—now!"

"Please let me have just a few days and I will pay you," pled the man. But the wicked servant refused, saying, "I will have you cast into jail until all you owe is paid to me."

Some bystanders, fellow servants, told the king, "Do you remember that servant whose enormous debt you forgave? We just saw him threaten our fellow servant over a small amount of money owed to him."

The king's anger flashed! He called for the servant to be brought to him and asked him why he wouldn't forgive his fellow servant just as the king had forgiven him. The king then put the man in jail and delivered him over to the tormentors until he could pay all that was due.

This parable reveals the two sides of forgiveness—the practical side, or what it means to forgive, and the personal side, or what forgiving will do for you and those whom you forgive. And finally, that parable speaks volumes about the manner in which your willingness to forgive affects your fellowship in prayer with the Father. Christ said, "So My heavenly Father also will do to you if each of you, from his heart, does not forgive his brother his trespasses" (Matt. 18:35).

THE PRACTICAL SIDE

What is forgiveness? As used in this parable, the word *forgive* means to send someone away or to go away yourself, *leaving all claims behind*. At its heart, forgiveness is not basically an act of the emotions. It is a deliberate, volitional decision by which you say, "This person is no longer indebted to me. I choose to hold no more claims against him or her."

In Jesus' day, those hearing the parable for the first time undoubtedly associated the king's forgiveness with a very specific picture. The king called the servant before a court witness in order to forgive him the debt. Proper documents were prepared in duplicate, one set for the forgiven man and one for the files of the kingdom. These documents recorded the name of the man, the name of the king, the amount the man owed, and the statement, "Forgiven!" or "Paid in full." The king signed them, then the man. Finally a representative sealed them. The forgiven man kept one copy, and the other was filed away.

There was a specific reason for following such a procedure. Imagine that some months later the king must contemplate a costly building project. As he considers the cost, his advisers counsel him, "We know where you can obtain the money for the project. Remember that servant with that enormous debt? Make him pay. He owes it to you."

Soon the man finds himself standing before the king. "But," he protests, "you forgave me for that!" Looking through the files, the court clerk confirms that at a specific time in the past the king had indeed forgiven the servant. The king might be disgusted, his anger might boil, but there is nothing he can do. Perhaps such a scene might even be repeated as time blurs the king's memory. But on each occasion he would return to the fact that he had forgiven his debtor.

Here is the point: Even if we decide to forgive someone, we might on future occasions be tempted to bring that person's case back into the courtroom of our emotions and try to demand payment all over again. But with the Holy Spirit's assistance, we will be able to recall that at a specific moment in the past we chose to forgive, and we have no further claim on the offending party.

When Satan tempts us to hold the forgiven person in our debt, we can say, "There is no sense in pursuing this. The record may be frayed and dog-eared from my repeated reference to it, but I do not need to drag it out. On a specific day in the past I chose to forgive, I relinquished all claims against this person, and I refuse to go back on my decision." That is forgiveness!

Forgiveness must be distinguished from other practices closely associated with it. *Forgiving does not mean, for instance, that we approve of another's actions.* Once a troubled young wife and mother asked whether forgiving her father for molesting her as a child meant that she accepted and approved of his perverted activities. I told her no, noting that Christ forgives us but does not approve of our sin.

Neither is forgiveness the same as reconciliation or restitution. It is wonderful when either of these happens. But if they had to precede forgiving, we could be hopelessly trapped in bitterness—if, for example, the offending party died before either could be accomplished. At the same time, forgiveness does, in fact, pave the way for both of these to occur.

Once, when speaking on this issue of forgiveness, I asked those who would choose to forgive to stand up as an indication of their intent. One man stood, grieving over the fact that his unforgiven brother had disappeared and he might never have the opportunity to share what was in his heart. But as he turned to be seated, he discovered his offending brother standing directly behind him. What a joyous reconciliation! And it happened because two men were willing to say, "As of this day, the debt is paid. I am owed nothing. I forgive!"

THE PERSONAL SIDE

But what does forgiveness do for the persons we forgive—and for us?

When we forgive someone, we remove ourselves as a controlling factor in that individual's behavior. No longer can that person say, "My life could be different, but he will not forgive me." Remember, when we refuse to forgive someone, we are retaining that person's case in *our* courtroom! We have yet to turn it over to God. We are saying in essence, "I have a higher standard of justice than God!"

Have you ever wondered why people who have committed injustice and wrong against us sometimes seem to prosper in this world? Perhaps an individual has mistreated us, and in our heart we might have said, "That does it! You have mistreated God's anointed, His innocent child. Now God is going to let the hammer fall!" But instead the offender prospers! He is driving a new car, he is living in a new house, and he may wear better clothes than we do! We protest, "Lord, *he* offended *me*. When are You going to let him have it?" And God gently reminds us, "You have not released him to Me yet! Quit trying to be judge and jury. Pray that I will treat him as graciously as you would want to be treated yourself."

Refusing to forgive is a subtle way of saying, "I am afraid that if I forgive this individual, God will not treat him as I think he should be treated." In contrast, the forgiving person says, "Dear God, I rest my case. That individual is Yours to deal with, not mine. I have no further claims. I set him free."

That is what forgiveness does for the person whom we forgive. We no longer give him or her an excuse for an improper response. But what will choosing to forgive some offense from our past do for us? Forgiveness has five positive results.

Release from Debt

When we refuse to forgive others, we also believe they deserve something more from us—a lecture, a cold shoulder, criticism, rudeness. We believe we should punish the offender, that we must somehow balance the scales. When we forgive, we are released from that debt—we are set free. Biblically, we owe the person nothing but love (Rom. 13:8).

Following his act of forgiveness, the king in Jesus' parable wanted to never again consider the servant his adversary. In fact, he hoped they could enjoy their restored fellowship. Only that servant's unwillingness to forgive a fellow servant brought him once again under the king's discipline.

Unforgiving people always feel it is necessary to get even. They sense there is an unpaid debt and they must set the record straight. But when we forgive, those feelings are removed, and fellowship can be restored. We are released from our unholy burden.

Reliance on the Lord

A second positive result of forgiveness is that it helps us to rely fully on the Lord. An unforgiving person subconsciously feels that others hold the key to his happiness and success. But when we forgive someone, we are saying God meets all of our needs. A forgiving spirit casts us totally on the resources of God!

The king could forgive the servant's debt because he did not need the man's money. The huge debt was not greatly urgent to him. Similarly, we can forgive other people for what we feel they owe us because we do not need it. We have more than enough because we have Christ.

When we say, "I will *not* forgive," we are saying, "Something is missing. The offending party holds the key to my joy. I need a certain something from someone on this earth, something that God above cannot provide."

But when we forgive, we are saying, "My God supplies *all* my need according to His riches in glory by Christ Jesus my Lord!" (see Phil. 4:19). By forgiving others, relinquishing any hold we have on them, we lean wholly on God. Such faith pleases the Lord greatly!

Restored Usefulness

Forgiveness will also restore us to ministry and fellowship. Unforgiving people are often perplexed when God takes them out of the mainstream of usefulness. Their theology is precise; we cannot fault them on their Christian character; everything about them seems exactly right. Yet they are on the shelf, rarely called upon by others, and in fact often avoided.

In reality, their refusal to forgive has brought them into a prison of uselessness. God has shut down their ministry and focused His attention on their discipline. Why should He exalt someone whose life is a direct contradiction to what He wants others to see in Himself— His love and forgiveness?

The unforgiving servant in the parable was put in prison, where he was totally ineffective, as is everyone who refuses to forgive. But when we forgive, our usefulness is restored.

Relief from Torment

Forgiveness brings deliverance from those who mistreat or oppress us. A person who will not forgive lives in agony. "And his master was angry, and delivered him to the torturers until he should pay all that was due to him." This kind of torment can come in various ways.

Some years ago I visited with a lady who had received the frightening diagnosis of a terminal illness. As we talked and I sought to comfort her, she said, "If God ever shows you anything about my situation, please let me know."

Later, during a time of Bible study and prayer, God directed me to Proverbs 17:22 with its solemn reminder that "a broken spirit dries the bones." Knowing that her illness was directly related to the failure of her bone marrow to produce life-giving blood, I decided to direct her attention to this passage of Scripture.

When we met, I asked her if some past event had brought great bitterness to her heart. She began to weep while recounting an event that had virtually devastated her. Choking back the tears, she asked why I thought such a thing existed in her past. I showed her Proverbs 17:22 and asked if she was willing to forgive.

In a moving prayer she chose to consider the offending party as no longer indebted to her. As a result, God moved remarkably in the life of this lady, restoring her to health and usefulness for many more years.

Ironically, the very people against whom we harbor a vindictive spirit usually do not know it. Unforgiving people suffer the most from their bitterness. When we forgive, we are released from such torture.

Recovered Fellowship with the Father

Forgiving does more than open the door for restored relationships with others. By forgiving others a believer regains fellowship with God. In His parable Jesus emphatically stated that a refusal to forgive others brings a similar response from God toward us: "So my Heavenly Father also will do to you if each of you, from his heart, does not forgive his brother his trespasses" (Matt. 18:35). The forgiving to which Jesus refers is not the forgiveness that brings salvation but fellowship instead.

A friend of mine once related that he had offended his wife with a critical remark, and she was finding it difficult to forgive him. "There's a chill in the air," he said as he tried to describe the atmosphere in his home. Many people sense a similar chill in their relationship with God. Their sins are covered by the death of Christ. But they know their behavior is not appropriate for blood-bought children of God; they are not living consistently with their calling. A major interruption of fellowship with God stems from an unforgiving spirit.

God is known for His forgiveness. How strange it must seem when we, the forgiven, refuse to forgive others. The Lord's parable shows the serious effects of such an unforgiving spirit. When we choose to forgive someone else, we are applying the grace of God to human lives. We are thus pleasing, serving, and worshiping Him.

FORGIVENESS AND PRAYER

The facets of forgiveness we have been examining closely relate to prayer. The failure to forgive results in the loss of the five personal benefits discussed above, each of which is crucial if we are to pray effectively. "If I regard iniquity in my heart, the LORD will not hear" (Ps. 66:18), and that includes the sin of refusing to forgive someone else. If we are not only to pray but to persevere in prayer, to pray effectively, we must be forgiving.

My father has always been my hero. Like his father before him, he served many years in gospel ministry. I have received his permission to relate the following story.

One day my father decided he would leave my mother, a devastating act with consequences that can be imagined only by those who have experienced such a tragedy.

At the time my parents were in their mid-sixties, having celebrated forty-three years of marriage, when he decided he would leave. I do not understand, nor did he, all the dynamics of the spiritual and moral dementia that brought about the divorce. I do know that even now he shakes his head in sad wonderment over what occurred. Today he cautions everyone he meets regarding the importance of "daily bread," regular intake of the Word of God. He says, "I have discovered that you cannot build up enough 'points' with God so that you can ever afford to simply coast in your spiritual life. The moment you set aside the Word of God, you become vulnerable to whatever Satan sets before you."

Before my own family departed for the mission field, I sensed the difficulties mounting in my father's life and tried desperately to do something about it. I vividly remember calling my parents before we boarded the plane in New York only to discover that my father had left my mother! I had previously counseled with many people whose parents had gone through divorce. But until that moment I never really understood the situation. If divorce deeply hurts a grown man, which it does, I cannot imagine what it does to a three-year-old or a nine-year-old or a fifteen-year-old or a college student!

Within months of his departure my father remarried and moved to a distant state. Communication, strained at best, was virtually nonexistent. We all sought to comfort and encourage my godly yet grieving mother, who struggled to understand how her beautiful family had been broken apart.

Several years after the divorce, my mother began to exhibit the early signs of Alzheimer's. A lovely, godly, wonderful woman attacked with Alzheimer's! I cried out, "God, this doesn't seem fair! She isn't the one who's supposed to have the problems! Why should my mother have to suffer so?"

One day I received a call from my brother, who lived very close to my mother. "Mother has had a cerebral hemorrhage," he said.

"She's in the hospital and is at the point of death. Come quickly." All the family gathered at her bedside to hear the doctor say, "There is really no way she can live. She is going to die—soon, I think, although we can never be certain about such things." When he said that, we could see my mother literally dig in, in spite of the fact that she lay there in a coma. We did not realize then all that God had in store for us over the next few weeks.

A week passed, then a second week. Toward the end of the second week, Mother stirred a little, and she uttered three words: "Want! Want! Want!" My brother, who was by her bedside, said, "Mother, what do you want? Do you want ice? Do you want a drink of water? Do you want your pillow changed? What do you want? Do you want to be turned?" When none of his suggestions seemed to satisfy her, he began to call the names of friends and family, finally asking, "Is it Dad?" She then uttered three more words: "Forgive! Forgive! Forgive!"

He replied, "Mother, we have forgiven him, and we know you have too." But there was no response. Once again my mother had lapsed into a coma.

The next day our family gathered around her bed, thinking our Mother was going to die anytime. As we sang, prayed, cried, and read the Word of God, the phone rang. It was my father, who had not spoken to my mother in almost two and a half years. Weeping, he said, "Can I speak to Mama?" I said, "Dad, she's in a coma." "Well," he said, "I need to talk to her."

When I put the phone to Mother's ear, her eyes opened, her body came to attention, tears ran from the corners of her eyes, and she said, "I forgive you. I love you."

I thought about a poem I had seen.

> He drew a circle that shut me out,
> Daunted, rebel—a thing to flout,
> But love and I had the wit to win,
> We drew a circle that shut him in.

Forgiveness has remarkable restorative power. For twenty-four hours my mother remained lucid. She said, "Isn't that something, Dad calling? You know, I have to witness for Jesus even more." Then she quietly slipped into a coma.

Several more weeks passed with Mother lying there in a coma. Dad called almost every day inquiring, "What do you think?" Finally we said, "Dad, we don't know what she's waiting for. Maybe she's waiting for you."

The next day our entire family, including my father, stood in a circle around her bed holding hands. In only a few days Mother peacefully went to be with the Lord.

> *But love and I had the wit to win,*
> *We drew a circle that shut him in.*

God used my mother's determined love and prayers and her forgiving spirit to restore relationships in our family. My father and his wife now live back "at home" surrounded by their relatives and friends. We have talked openly and candidly about the events that led to the divorce and subsequent marriage. While no one can undo the events of the past, God has shown us the sufficiency of His grace. Since then the Lord has used my father on more than one occasion to dissuade others from making the same tragic choices he made. And all of us in the family share a genuine God-given love for one another.

My mother understood. "Forgive! Forgive! Forgive!" Then we can pray and keep on praying, serve and keep on serving, worship and keep on worshiping.

QUESTIONS FOR REFLECTION AND PRAYER

1. Is there anyone whom you need to forgive? Ask God to bring such persons to mind right now. Why have you not forgiven him or her or them? Will you choose to do so today? Talk with God further about all this now.

2. Release from debt—reliance on the Lord—restored usefulness—relief from torment—recovered fellowship with the Father—which of these benefits of forgiving others means the most to you?

Why? Which do you need the most these days? Why? Discuss all this with God now.

3. How do forgiveness and prayer relate to each other? How has this been true in your life? Are your prayers being hindered by bitterness at this time? Converse with God honestly and specifically about this now.

13

PRAYING DURING
THE HARD TIMES OF LIFE

*Count it all joy when you
fall into various trials.*

JAMES 1:2

WE WERE SEATED IN A SMALL CIRCLE on the second floor of a church in a developing but still destitute far-eastern nation. Looking out the window I could see a jumble of thatched roofs atop tiny huts jammed together. Competing smells from cooking fires, incense, stagnant water, and refuse wafted along the slight breeze that brought minimal relief from the heat.

This neighborhood on the outskirts of a major city was fortunate to have electricity delivered by a tangled web of wires that only added to the visual confusion. Overhead, prized ceiling fans vibrated and squeaked in a losing fight against the relentless heat and humidity.

But the faces in that circle constantly called my attention back to the room—the faces of pastors, church planters, and leaders of congregations in a country that still had only an uncomfortable alliance with Christianity. With the material that became this chapter in mind, I listened as the believers shared the prayer needs of their churches. One leader had a price on his head because he dared to preach about Jesus. Another asked prayer for strength—malnutrition was making it difficult for him to visit each of his ten preaching points. A man with an artificial limb (one leg had been blown away by a land mine) asked for prayer as he worked with the handicapped who gathered regularly at the base of a nearby Buddhist temple.

They had all suffered in one way or another as they sought to bring gospel truth to a land darkened by centuries of heathen worship. The combined forces of war, paganism, poverty, and persecution were overwhelming to my western mind. Yet, that room abounded with joy, love, and laughter. These were people who knew how to pray victoriously in difficult situations.

Their experience was not unlike that addressed by James, a half-brother of Jesus who was considered the senior pastor in the church in Jerusalem. In his epistle, part of Holy Scripture, he was writing to believers who had been dispersed throughout the Mediterranean world by the heavy hand of Roman rule. Persecution, famine, harassment, misunderstanding, estrangement from family and friends—this was the road the church trod just a few years after the ascension of Christ. Each knock at the door might mean food for another meal, or arrest and imprisonment. They could never be sure.

James wrote to these "brethren" (Jas. 1:2) about "various trials" (1:2)—tough times. He did not need to define the term; they were all going through the experience. So James opened his letter with instruction on how to face difficult circumstances. He taught them *how to pray about hard situations*.

WHO, ME?

Why are we surprised when trying dilemmas knock at our door? We tell God with puzzled voice and furrowed brow, "You must be kidding! I didn't become a believer with this in mind. This is not my idea of the 'abundant life'!" But God knows exactly what He is doing in each of our lives.

God assures us that He is powerfully and lovingly at work for our good and His glory in every life situation. "And we know that all things work together for good to those who love God, for those who are the called according to His purpose" (Rom. 8:28). "Be anxious for nothing, but in everything by prayer and supplication, with thanksgiving, let your requests be made known to God; and the peace of God, which surpasses all understanding, will guard your hearts and minds through Christ Jesus" (Phil. 4:6-7). He is sufficient in every circumstance; He has a beneficent purpose for each day's events.

However, since we sometimes cannot clearly see His ultimate purpose, *our immediate goal must be to cooperate with His plan and to keep trusting Him.* Prayer is an essential component of this ongoing relationship. Paul reminds us, "Work out your own salvation with fear and trembling; for it is God who works in you both to will and to do for His good pleasure" (Phil. 2:12-13). In times of serenity and of struggle, we need to cooperate with God, being confident that He knows what He is doing with us.

Private Wars

We all face trying circumstances; we all understand the "various trials" about which James writes. Of course, our particular situation may seem small in comparison to others'; but it is *our* situation and therefore a definite concern for us! As a friend of mine says, "The difference between major surgery and minor surgery is simple: yours is minor, mine is major!" Each person faces his or her own private wars.

Several years ago I returned from an embattled part of the globe grieving over the hard situations faced by believers there. The following Sunday I attempted to draw our congregation into the circle of concern by vividly detailing the hardships faced by the small band of believers overseas. As I preached, I could see that some in the congregation were finding it difficult to care about battles being fought 5,000 miles away. They had just come from their own war zones—at home, at work, at school. We all have our battles.

Life is full of hard situations. That is why James's letter was not written as a contingency plan. He did not say, "*If* you have trials." He gave solid advice enabling proper responses to actual events—"*when* you fall into various trials." Difficult circumstances are a reality for all of us. Because they are inevitable, we must be ready with proper, godly responses to those situations. "Consider it all as a cause for rejoicing," James urges the perplexed followers of Christ.

A notable characteristic of this letter is that it says less *about* Christ than any other New Testament epistle, and yet it sounds more *like* Christ! James's words are reminiscent of Christ's in the Sermon on the Mount: "Blessed are you when they revile and persecute you, and say all kinds of evil against you falsely, for My sake. Rejoice and be exceedingly glad" (Matt. 5:11-12).

Is our Savior asking us to *pretend* to be happy? Is this some type of mental gymnastic designed to keep the Enemy off guard and ourselves fooled? Hardly! James tells us that God's loving purpose for tough times comes only as we acknowledge what He can accomplish through them—patience and mature faith.

Picture a scowling coach standing eyeball to eyeball with an intimidated athlete in soaked workout sweats. "We *are* having fun, aren't we, Jones?" shouts the coach. "Y-Y-Y-essir!" stammers Jones, out of breath from running wind sprints. "Good," screams the coach, "because you're going to be doing this twice a day for the next two weeks!"

Football players and other athletes are familiar with such grueling ordeals. Considering how hard such experiences are, why do players keep volunteering season after season? Because they know that the purpose of the grueling exercise is *conditioning*, without which teams just do not win. Weeks later an exhausted player coming to the sidelines might say, "Now *this* is fun, isn't it coach?"

No *chastening seems to be joyful for the present, but painful; nevertheless, afterward it yields the peaceable fruit of righteousness to those who have been trained by it.*
—HEBREWS 12:11

We can approach every hard situation in life with an attitude of joyful expectation if we understand that God is at work, helping us grow through exercise and exertion, developing our spiritual muscles, preparing us for even greater usefulness. As we stay in touch with Him through prayer throughout the process, we can maintain a healthy perspective and a steady confidence in Him.

What Next?

Once we accept the fact that the hard situations in our lives are for our good and His glory, we can prayerfully and aggressively seek to cooperate with His plan. It is imperative that we remember that *God always operates according to principle*. And His principles are immutable; they are flawless and unchanging. In every situation of life His standards and directives can guide our behavior.

Not all of us face the exact same hard situations. I have known some people whose difficulties were monetary. Trials left them virtually destitute, with no apparent way out of their financial sinkholes. Sadly, some of these folk abandoned any pretense of faith, turning away from God and His Word. They became tight-fisted, hard, bitter. And there has been no apparent change in their situation to this day, except that it has become more desperate.

In contrast, others going through financial trials turned to God's principles of stewardship. Realizing that He owns everything and they own nothing, they sought God's will in the Scriptures. They began practicing the tithe and saw God open up windows of blessing (see Mal. 3:10-12). (One man testified that he literally tithed his way off of welfare.) As their faith grew, they began practicing the law of the harvest (2 Cor. 9:6-8), and God has blessed them accordingly.

For others, a strained marriage was the problem. On any given Sunday morning I see in our congregation I lead several men whose wives applied God's principles to their troubled marriages. Some of them had for many years attempted to be the spiritual leaders in their homes, rationalizing that their husbands were unsaved and uncooperative. Later, as God dealt with them, they saw the importance of placing that responsibility squarely on the shoulders of their husbands and refusing to usurp that role. God used that obedience to His principles in a dramatic fashion and reached the hearts of their husbands.

Whatever the difficult situations we face, however trying they might be, whatever the root causes are, help and resolution will come only as we surrender to the Lord and His purposes for our lives. We must trust and obey Him.

What if we do not know what God expects us to do about our

particular situation? "If any of you lacks wisdom, let him *ask of God*, who gives to all liberally and without reproach, and it will be given to him" (Jas. 1:5). What should we do? *Pray.* Not only does God answer our prayers for wisdom, He answers them generously and without rebuking us for asking!

I have a friend who has had a successful home construction business in a large city for many years. As a young man, he was taught by his father to steal and drink. Later he entered the Navy, from which he ultimately received a dishonorable discharge. Possessing only a fifth-grade education, he went to work as a carpenter on a framing crew. But God's grace reached this man's heart, and soon he came to salvation through faith in Christ.

With the help of his wife he began to pray for wisdom about the direction his life should take. One day he told me with tears, "God spoke to me while I was framing a house. He said if I could frame a house, I could also build one. Later He guided me into development and sales. This is all His business." Following the Lord's guidance, depending on Him for needed wisdom, this man has found fullness and usefulness.

HOW TO ASK

When we seek God's wisdom during hard times, we are to ask "in faith, with no doubting" (Jas. 1:6). In other words, we are to approach the Father with confidence, knowing He has instructed and invited us to do so. "Doubting" is pictured as restlessness on our part—"like a wave of the sea driven and tossed by the wind." Wavering prayer results in no response on God's part.

A man whose wife had left him a short time earlier stopped by my office one day to say he was on his way to his lawyer's office. "I'm going to file for divorce," he said with an air of resignation. When I protested and encouraged him to keep praying for his wife, he laughed. "Look," he said, "for two weeks I've been a good boy—prayed, read the Bible, come to church. But she still won't come home. So what's the use?"

Doubting prayer gives God a shot at the situation but stands ready to take over if He doesn't come through in short order. Such prayer is like digging up seeds every day to see if the vegetables or flowers are growing as they should. In contrast, the psalmist wrote, "Commit your way to the LORD, trust also in Him, and He will bring it to pass" (Ps. 37:5). We must give it to Him, leave it with Him, and let Him do the work. Faith in God includes a willingness to wait until He clearly shows us the principle upon which we are to act. Once we see the path He means for us, we can aggressively cooperate with Him and keep serving Him until He brings about the results He intended.

Horticulturists know how best to grow a large tree with roots deep enough to sustain it through a storm. "Don't baby it," they say. "If you give it too much water and nutrients, it will become a big tree with an inadequate root system. Hard times develop deep roots."

Remember the circle of prayer warriors in that strife-torn third-world country that I mentioned at the beginning of this chapter? Listen to their testimonies. Listen to their prayers. *Hard times develop deep roots.* Rejoice! Pray! Abide in Him and His purposes!

QUESTIONS FOR REFLECTION AND PRAYER

1. What trials are you currently facing? Do you believe God is using them for your good? Why or why not? What benefits could possibly come from these difficult circumstances? Talk to God about this now.

2. Are you staying in communication with God about your present trials, or are you attempting to work them out on your own? Why? Do you find it easy or hard to ask God for wisdom? Why? Review past situations in which you asked for God's wisdom and He answered. Praise Him for those times now, and pray for wisdom and strength for current and future trials.

3. Do you sometimes ask God for wisdom and guidance but doubt that He will come through for you? Why? What can you do to doubt less and trust more? Discuss this with God honestly right now.

14

Praying for
a "Blessing"

*He blessed and broke and gave
the loaves to the disciples.*

Matthew 14:19

DO YOUR PRAYERS FREQUENTLY include the request that God "bless" someone or some church or organization? What do you mean by this? Are you simply asking God to do something "good" or to make something "work out all right"? Or is there a deeper significance to this request that, if you grasped it, would add new earnestness to your praying?

In the biblical sense, a blessing is *a sovereign act of God by which he causes someone or something to supernaturally produce more than would be naturally possible*. When we ask the Lord, for instance, to bless a certain missionary, we are asking God to give him the ability to accomplish more than is humanly possible. Praying that God bless an offering indicates a desire for God to superintend the use of that money so that it accomplishes more than it would if dispensed on the basis of human cleverness. A prisoner of war might ask God to bless meager rations so his life can be sustained on a diet that is totally inadequate. God's blessing on a preacher or on the message he delivers results in an effective ministry that cannot be explained on the basis of human logic or talents.

Living below the standards of God's blessing shows the world nothing more than that which can be attained by human effort. We must have the blessing of God on our lives, homes, jobs, churches, and ministries if the world is to fully understand who Christ is and what He can do in human lives. But how do we obtain the blessing of God?

The principles of praying for a blessing are seen in Jesus' miraculously feeding more than 5,000 people with five loaves and two fishes, as recorded in Matthew 14:15-21:

> When it was evening, His disciples came to Him, saying, "This is a deserted place, and the hour is already late. Send the multitudes away, that they may go into the villages and buy themselves food." But Jesus said unto them, "They do not need to go away. You give them something to eat." And they said to Him, "We have here only five loaves and two fish." He said, "Bring them here to Me." Then He commanded the multitudes to sit down on the grass. And He took the five loaves and the two fish, and looking up to heaven, He blessed and broke and gave the loaves to the disciples, and the disciples gave to the multitudes. So they all ate and were filled, and they took up twelve baskets full of the fragments that remained. Now those who had eaten were about five thousand men, besides women and children.

UNLIMITED BY THE SIZE OF OUR NEED

Imagine the scene and its apparent hopelessness! A late hour, a deserted place, and over 5,000 people needing to be fed! The disciples, overwhelmed with the magnitude of such a responsibility, requested that Jesus "Send the multitudes away, that they may go into the villages and buy themselves food" (v. 15). But Jesus was determined to prove that there is no limit to what may be accomplished when we have God's blessing.

We often view situations as either too large for our faith or too small for God to bother with. Satan will never say to us, "That's just the right size for God to handle." He loves to make us think that before we approach God, we should determine if the solution to our problem is within the realm of possibility.

When Abraham met with the Lord in the plains of Mamre he was given this message:

> *"I will certainly return to you according to the time of life, and behold, Sarah your wife shall have a son." . . . Now Abraham and Sarah were old, well advanced in age; and Sarah had passed the age of childbearing. Therefore Sarah laughed within herself, saying, "After I have grown old, shall I have pleasure, my lord being old also?" And the* LORD *said to Abraham, "Why did Sarah laugh, saying, 'Shall I surely bear a child, since I am old?' Is anything too hard for the* LORD?"
>
> —GENESIS 18:10-14

Why was Sarah so astounded by this message from the Lord? The Lord had told Abraham on a previous occasion, "And I will bless her and also give you a son by her" (Gen. 17:16). Like us, she was reluctant to claim the blessing in the face of seemingly insurmountable odds. But God's blessing is not limited by the size of our need. "Is anything too hard for the LORD?"

UNLIMITED BY THE CAUSE OF OUR NEED

The disciples urged Jesus to send the people away so they could buy food for themselves. But Jesus said, "They do not need to go away. You give them something to eat" (Matt. 14:16). Apparently the disciples had been given the responsibility for feeding the multitude, but the situation had sneaked up on them. A desperate attempt to gather sufficient provisions resulted in a meager supply—"We have here only five loaves and two fish" (v. 17). Is it possible that the predicament was caused by their carelessness? No matter! "Bring them here to Me," the Lord said about the insufficient food supply (v. 18). Certainly we sometimes fall short in our responsibilities as Christ's disciples and ministers, but He, in His mercy, more than makes up for our deficiency and uses us to feed large multitudes.

Many people labor under the misconception that prayer is available or effective only in situations they did not cause or affect. "I would ask God to rescue me," they say, "but I brought the problem on myself.

It's a result of my own rebellion and carelessness, so . . ." But, praise God, that is precisely when He is most joyful about our approach to His throne of grace. When we are convicted of the hopelessness of our humanity and come to Him for help, acknowledging our limitations and flaws, He welcomes us with open arms of undeserved favor and persistent compassion.

A Bible verse we considered earlier, Colossians 2:6, says: "As you therefore have received Christ Jesus the Lord, so walk in Him." Only when we finally became convinced that we were responsible for our sin and that no works of righteousness would ever save us did we turn to Christ in faith and receive Him as Savior. Our walk with Christ must include a day-by-day acknowledgment of personal failure *and* a day-by-day trust in the sufficiency of His grace.

God's blessings are not limited by the cause of our need. Otherwise, we would have to live under the constant strain of trying to earn right standing with God so we could pray to Him.

UNLIMITED BY THE AVAILABLE RESOURCES

I can picture the disciples taking Christ aside so others would not see their looks of distress or hear their worried conversation. Jesus had said, "Give them something to eat," and their hearts had melted. Now as they circled around the Lord, they cast furtive glances first at the crowd, then at one another. "You tell him," they each seemed to be saying. Finally one of them unwrapped the cloth around a small basket. "We have here only five loaves and two fish." Surely this would convince the Lord to send the multitude away.

But God's blessing is not limited to the human resources available. Otherwise He would not be God! The growth and ministry of many churches, and of many individual believers, has been impeded by a failure to learn this lesson. Too often we make our plans on the basis of what we think *we* can do rather than on what *God* can do through us as we obey Him.

Christian witness would be immensely more effective and potent if church leaders and committees would be more occupied with seeking the mind of God than with the results of past human effort.

J. Hudson Taylor, founder of the China Inland Mission, insisted, "God's work done God's way receives God's supply." Can you imagine planning the Israelites' journey from Egypt to the Promised Land on the basis of either the previous year's receipts or a projected wilderness economy? Instead, the people of God simply had to trust and obey one day at a time, confidently depending on God to be all they needed, no matter what trials or enemies they faced. It is the same with us.

Many Christians fail to ask for God's blessing because they assume it must come through an existing channel. Is that how God worked during the forty years in the desert? The sovereign God can work and supply however He wishes. Again the issue is never what we can do, but rather what we will allow God to do through us. We should not be discouraged because we cannot see how God will bring about a needed blessing. "It is the glory of God to conceal a matter" (Prov. 25:2). "But seek first the kingdom of God and His righteousness," said our Lord, "and all these things shall be added to you" (Matt. 6:33).

APPROPRIATING GOD'S BLESSING

"Bring them here to Me," Jesus said of the loaves and fishes, and shortly afterward they all received sufficient food, with leftovers to spare. How was this miraculous feast given and distributed? Matthew 14:19 tells us, "Then He commanded the multitudes to sit down on the grass. And He took the five loaves and the two fish, and looking up to heaven, He blessed and broke and gave the loaves to the disciples, and the disciples gave to the multitudes." What are the keys to receiving God's blessing for a specific situation? Jesus' example is most enlightening.

Jesus assessed the situation. He seated the people in an orderly fashion (compare Mark 6:39-40). He obviously knew the exact extent of the need and what it would take to meet it. Furthermore, He took the loaves and fish in hand so He would know exactly what resources were available to feed all those people.

Many people are vaguely aware that they need God's blessing, but they have never taken the time to accurately assess their situation.

Interestingly, many who were known for receiving great answers to prayer (for example, George Müller, J. Hudson Taylor, and David Brainerd) carefully recorded their needs and God's response. They saw much of what came their way, small or large, as part of God's answer to their prayers.

Jesus sought the mind of God. He looked to heaven (Matt. 14:19), recognizing God as the source of supply, being willing to conform to the Father's revealed will. We too must seek a word from God—not only in regard to His willingness to bless, but also in regard to the manner of behavior He can bless.

Back in Old Testament times, at Meribah, God assured Moses of His desire to provide water for the Israelites. He also told Moses how He wanted him to behave: "Speak to the rock before their eyes, and it will yield its water; thus you shall bring water out of the rock" (Num. 20:8). In his response, Moses acknowledged God's desire to bless but was not willing to conform to His prescribed pattern of behavior. Instead of speaking to the rock, Moses struck it, as he had (rightly) done earlier. This act of angry disobedience cost Moses his entrance into the Promised Land of Canaan.

God could have provided for the hungry multitude in Jesus' day in many ways. But He wanted Christ to divide the loaves and fish among the seated crowd. Jesus obeyed, and the people received a miracle-feast. We too must seek the mind of God and act accordingly, obeying the Father to whom we belong.

Jesus blessed God and requested a blessing on the loaves and fish (Matt. 14:19). In the original language of the New Testament the word for "blessing" indicates an act of praise, consecration, and petition. In this passage we read simply, "He blessed," and this evidently included praise to the Father and a request that the loaves and fish be consecrated to God's use so that those meager resources would provide sufficient food for the multitude.

As we pray for God's blessing, our prayers should similarly include praise, consecration, and petition. We are asking God to cause someone or something to accomplish in a supernatural fashion more than would be naturally possible. As we do that, praising Him builds our faith; consecration, offering ourselves to Him to use however He wishes, settles the issue of lordship and opens the door for making an effective petition.

Jesus acted in obedience to the Father. Once He had prayed and received God's guidance regarding the present situation, He acted on what He had been told. After the blessing, Jesus "broke and gave the loaves to the disciples; and the disciples gave to the multitude" (v. 19). Jesus Christ not only asked for the blessing but was actively involved in its provision and distribution.

Many Christians ask the Lord to bless certain individuals or activities but forget that God may want *them* to be channels of blessing. It is one thing, for instance, to ask God to bless a missionary. It is another matter to say, "Lord, if I am to be the channel for Your blessing to this missionary, show me, and I will act accordingly." The blessed food still had to be passed throughout the multitude. Asking God to bless an evangelistic crusade is appropriate, but we must personally share the Gospel with needy individuals. If in any circumstance we are to see God's intended blessing become a reality, we must act in faith according to His revealed will.

When the whole multitude had been fed—5,000 men plus women and children—twelve full baskets were left over! God not only hears prayer, God not only provides, God not only reaches out to those who need His help—He does all that with incredible generosity and abundance! How desperately the world needs to see God's blessing in this fashion. Think about that the next time you pray for a blessing!

QUESTIONS FOR REFLECTION AND PRAYER

1. What current needs in your life do you sometimes think are beyond God's ability or concern? Why do you occasionally feel this way? What can you do to avoid such misconceptions of God? Talk to God about this now.

2. What do you want to happen in your life (in your family, your church, your workplace, your community) that goes beyond what human resources can accomplish? Are you depending on yourself or on God to bring this about? Why? With what results? How does your thinking on this matter need to change? Pray about this right now.

3. Assessing the situation—seeking God's mind—blessing God and the available resources—obeying the Father—which of these aspects of receiving God's blessing is hardest for you? Why? What can you do to allow God to help you be more Christlike in these areas? Discuss this in detail with God now.

15

PRAYING AWAY
THE CURSE OF WORDS

But no man can tame the tongue.
It is an unruly evil, full of deadly poison.

JAMES 3:8

I WAS DISGUSTED WITH MYSELF for accepting a speaking engagement in the far southwest corner of our state. Since the round trip would involve over six hours of driving, I would arrive home well after midnight—no problem except I needed to be fresh for a breakfast meeting only a few hours later. A foolish dilemma, and yet now I look back on that time as a significant turning point in my life.

In our church I was then preaching a series of messages on the Ten Commandments. The coming week's message was on the ninth commandment: "You shall not bear false witness against your neighbor" (Exod. 20:16). As I drove along, I meditated on Scripture passages citing the power and problems associated with the tongue.

I recalled that over the years I had been the recipient of strong doses of verbal encouragement. For example, my parents regularly handed out generous amounts of positive affirmation. But it occurred to me that in addition to such valuable encouragement, I had allowed five statements to exert a profoundly negative effect on my life. Two of these were spoken directly to me and were prefaced with "You're just like . . ." or "You will always . . ." Three of the statements I had overheard from others but nevertheless received them as unquestionably true. They did to my spiritual life what "passive smoke" does to us physically. Drawn in and absorbed, those statements had deadly effects.

What the exact statements were is not important. What is important is that *I had become the unwitting victim of the curse of words.* Even worse, I found myself fulfilling these malignant prophecies in surprising ways. That night on a lonely stretch of Oklahoma highway, God showed me how to break the curse of words, a dramatic turning point for me.

The effect was nothing short of profound. By the time I arrived back home, I was enjoying a remarkable, personal revival. With my voice hoarse from singing God's praises, I tried to tell my wife what had happened. The next evening I gathered our family to share what the Lord had revealed to me about breaking free from the curse of words. When I questioned whether they understood, my wife and children, one by one, often with tears, related that they had carried similar negative thoughts in their own hearts.

My wife recounted an incident in her childhood when she was told she would "never amount to anything." One daughter recounted in vivid detail a moment in Africa when she tried to get me away from an international phone call because she had seen a snake in our yard. In my exasperation I had said, "I could just shoot you!" and from that moment she had secretly questioned her value as a family member. Another had been told by a friend that she was "dense" for not getting the punch line of a humorous story. Because of that experience she began to question her intellectual abilities. Still another had been told by a jealous classmate that she only had friends because her father was a pastor. My son said that someone once told him his role in life was to keep everyone laughing, a remark that made him feel inferior and insignificant.

God met with our family around the table that evening. As I shared with them what you will read in the following pages, He brought us to a time of prayer that gave birth to a deep sense of revival, the effects of which continue to this day. He gave us sufficient grace to break the curse of words. Even this stronghold can be demolished as we pray to our awesome God (see 2 Cor. 10:4-5)!

As we have seen, the prayer life is not a spiritual discipline that is isolated from other areas of our lives. Time in the Word, compassionate witness, a dependence on God rather than ourselves, fasting, growing faith, receiving and giving forgiveness—these and many other aspects of the believer's life touch and are touched by our practice of prayer or the lack of it. In this chapter we will examine a deadly sin that many of us have committed and by which many of us have been victimized. Prayer is an essential element of renunciation of and deliverance from destructive words.

THE POWER OF WORDS

James tells us that words exert control in the same way a bit in the mouth of a horse controls that animal (Jas. 3:3). Many of us can testify to the big impact of little words—sometimes for good, sometimes for harm. Words are powerful, affecting all our lives positively or negatively. Consider, for example, the statement that so profoundly challenged Dwight L. Moody: "The world has yet to see what God can do with the life of a man totally committed to Him." Those words were to Moody like the rudders of great ships that "although they are so large and are driven by fierce winds . . . are turned by a very small rudder" (Jas. 3:4).

It is wonderful when words encourage or offer a positive challenge. But what about words that arouse bitter feelings or negative and fearful thoughts? Such words tend to enslave us in one way or another. Witness the exasperated, young wife who screams at her husband, "Don't you ever tell me I'm just like my mother! She used to say we were alike, and I hated her for it!" Though she justifies her reaction, she also knows she does indeed bear a chilling resemblance to a mother she would rather forget.

Reader's Digest has for many years carried a brief vocabulary test in each issue, "It Pays to Increase Your Word Power." Words do have awesome power. "The tongue," says James, "is a little member and boasts great things" (Jas. 3:5). Whether used for persuasion or putdowns, witness or criticism, encouragement or intimidation, words are potent!

THE AWFUL PROBLEM WITH WORDS

Words are powerful, but unfortunately they do not always have a beneficent effect. "See how great a forest a little fire kindles" (Jas. 3:5). Words do not always bring out the best in us. In fact, sometimes they elicit the worst and even wreak broad destruction.

As a young pastor, I was excited about attending the annual convention of our denomination. I knew that many of the men I most admired would be present. But a chance encounter with three of them left a negative impression on my life over which I only gained victory when I learned to break the curse of words. The encounter took place in the baggage claim area of a large airport. Neither of the men, to this day, is aware that I overheard their conversation.

They were discussing a Christian brother who had experienced a manner of success but was at the time struggling in a difficult situation. It seemed his rising star was now on the descent. Almost as an aside, one man said, "It has been my experience that if a man has it [whatever *it* is] and loses it, he never gets it again." The poisonous secondary smoke of that statement penetrated deep into my soul. Years later, while undergoing a time of personal spiritual struggle, I erroneously assumed that my life would never again be blessed by God as it had been in the past. The curse of words was at work.

We should heed the warnings of James about this area of our lives. Four evil forces seem to characterize the tongue.

The tongue is "a world of iniquity . . . it defiles the whole body, and sets on fire the course of nature; and it is set on fire by hell" (Jas. 3:6). Our tongues, our habits of speech, are tied to our hearts, which are also centers of iniquity. That is why, no matter how gracious we try to be with our words, the ultimate result of talking too much is sin (Prov. 10:19). All of us regret saying too much at one time or another.

The tongue is characterized by insubordination. While living in Africa, a friend took me on a hunt for Cape buffalo, one of the most feared of African game. After accomplishing our objective, we took a buffalo calf back to his ranch and turned it loose in a pen. For several weeks my friends attempted to domesticate that Cape buffalo calf but with no success. "What I've always heard is true," he lamented. "Cape buffalo can't be tamed!"

James noted that "every kind of beast and bird, of reptile and creatures of the sea, is tamed and has been tamed by mankind. But no man can tame the tongue" (Jas. 3:7-8). We can never afford to unleash the tongue and let it run free. Like the Cape buffalo, it will find someone to attack. Sometimes it will even turn on us!

The tongue is filled with infection. "It is an unruly evil, full of deadly poison" (Jas. 3:8). We would never knowingly allow someone to plunge a poison-filled syringe into our veins. In fact, we would do everything possible to resist such treatment. Yet we often unwittingly become infected by the poison that drips from the tongue of others. It is not enough to simply dislike what others say. Unless we properly immunize our spirit, such words can become venom that debilitates our effectiveness and drains away our joy.

I remember hearing a prison inmate describe his father's constant verbal attacks. Words like "useless," "obnoxious," "a bother," "killing your mother," and "driving me to an early grave" lacerated the prisoner's soul. "I know it was wrong of him to talk that way," he said shaking his head sadly, "and I thought if I got away from home, he couldn't hurt me with his words anymore. But he was right. I'm of no use to anyone." The poison had done its damage!

The tongue is evil in its inconsistency. The tongue will say anything! "Out of the same mouth proceed blessing and cursing," laments James (3:10). He notes that in the same breath we "bless God . . . and curse men, who have been made in the similitude of God" (v. 9). This, he continues, is contrary to the very laws of nature (vv. 11-12).

Several years ago I took a young man from our church to a local golf course, where we were asked to join another twosome. We were both shocked at the foul language of the other two men. Every shot was accompanied with an expletive. I was about to confront them when one of the men asked about my business. "I'm a pastor," I responded and told him about our church. With red face, the man noted that he was an active member and former chairman of the deacons at his church (a large, well-known congregation).

For the balance of the afternoon this man tried to convince us of his spirituality. A few weeks later he was pictured in a local newspaper as a large benefactor of a local Christian institution. My young friend clipped the article from the paper and sent it to me with the comment, "There is a lesson here somewhere, but I'm not sure what it is." The lesson is, apart from walking closely with Christ, the tongue is inconsistent, sometimes putting God first, sometimes putting self first.

BREAKING THE CURSE OF WORDS

We each might be able to think of specific words that have done or are now doing great damage in our lives. What they are causing us to think or do is destructive. It may feel like these words from the past have a stranglehold on our future that cannot be overcome. But no matter how convinced of that certainty we are, victory is available! How can we break the curse of words? God has placed three powerful weapons at our disposal. And in our battle to break the curse of words, those weapons are to be wielded through prayer—ongoing, persevering, confident, honest, passionate prayer.

Weapon #1: The Word of God

The account of Joseph's pilgrimage (Genesis 37—50) is a remarkable testimony to the power of God in a man's life. Scorned by his brothers, sold into slavery, falsely accused by his master's wife, forgotten in prison, Joseph had every human excuse to lose hope, become bitter, and harbor resentment. But Joseph was gripped by a truth that exceeded human reason. In spite of all that happened to him, Joseph knew from the age of seventeen that he would one day be instrumental in the rescue of his family. He held on to that conviction, never sinking to the petty behavior of his brothers, a behavior that would have forfeited his ability to be their deliverer. That conviction, no doubt, sustained him during those long nights in a cold prison.

It is so easy to accept what others say about us but overlook what God's Word says about us. When I first began to practice the truths discussed in this chapter, I shared them with a close friend in the ministry. His reputation as a pastor was impeccable, though those close to him knew there was a chink in his ministerial armor. He was a workaholic, always at everyone's beck and call; he was driven by the constant fear that he would overlook someone in need. For years his family had rarely gone on vacations lasting scarcely more than a week. "I don't like being away from my congregation," he would say. But the years, the burden, and the hours were taking their toll physically and spiritually.

One day when we were driving together to an engagement in a neighboring state, I shared with him about breaking the curse of words. A long, contemplative silence finally ended as he related how as a young student associate to a busy pastor, he'd overheard a conversation that set his behavioral course. Two secretaries were complaining about their pastor's frequent absence. One then mentioned my friend, saying, "He doesn't know much about preaching, but at least he's always here." "I concluded," he said, "that all I had to offer was just being there all the time. And I have worn myself out trying to live up to those words."

I shared with my friend the first principle in breaking the curse of words: *The truth about us is what God says about us—and nothing else.* Sincere conversation with God—sharing our inner hurts and self-doubts, listening to His assurances of our value in Christ—is healing and transforming.

Every statement about us must be measured, first of all, by the Word of God. Does God's Word say we can never have victory over a besetting sin? Or that we are useless? Or that we do not fit into His future plans? Does God's Word say that we can never again experience the fullness of His Spirit or the joy of His presence? Of course not!

Any statement or idea or criticism should be brought to the Word of the Lord, then cast down and held captive if it does not precisely agree with His will or opinion. Paul reminds us that "the weapons of our warfare are not carnal but mighty in God for pulling down strongholds, *casting down arguments and every high thing that exalts itself against the knowledge of God, bringing every thought into captivity to the obedience of Christ*" (2 Cor. 10:4-5).

While in prison Joseph must have brought thoughts of anger, bitterness, and revenge into captivity to the knowledge of God. Years later when his brothers fell in fear at his feet he could say, "You meant evil against me; but God meant it for good" (Gen. 50:20).

I once found myself growing cynical, critical, and caustic. A friend of mine faced me down about my attitude. "What's happening to you?" he asked. "Well," I responded, "I've been mulling over some things that were said about me recently." He answered, "Why don't you quit mulling over what those men said recently and start mulling over what God says about you today!" Great advice!

Any statement that will not pass the test of God's Word must be rejected outright. Like Jesus on the mount of temptation, we must answer accusations from the Devil and others with "It is written!" May we each maintain a faithful practice of prayer and abide in the Word of God, continually submitting ourselves to what God has to say about and to us.

Weapon #2: The Character of Jesus

God is at work in the life of every believer, conforming him to the image of His dear Son (Rom. 8:29). He is working in us "both to will and to do for His good pleasure" (Phil. 2:13). We are "His workmanship" (Eph. 2:10). He will one day present us to Himself as part of His "glorious church, not having spot or wrinkle or any such thing . . . holy and without blemish" (Eph. 5:27). God says that is who we are in Christ.

The passages of Scripture quoted above were penned by the apostle Paul, who endured constant criticism. The Jews considered him a traitor. The government considered him a nuisance. Those who in part owed their lives to him were often his fiercest critics. "You don't keep your word." "You don't love us." "You are too strict." "You are too loose." "You are too weak." "You are too strong." Paul well knew how much words can hurt—long-term! Yet he was content to run the race as a bondslave of Christ, knowing that his Lord had the final say as to his character and conduct (2 Tim 4:6-8).

If God is at work in our lives (and He is), we should never accept as the final word any human assessment that is not consistent with the character and word of Christ. To assume, for instance, that we will *never* improve in a specific area or *never* gain victory over a specific sin or *never* be where God wants us is to conclude that God is no longer at work in our lives, conforming us to the image of Christ. But He is! Sometimes we need to remind ourselves and our adversary of that important fact.

Constructive criticism from appropriate sources is always helpful if seen in the light of this truth. I remember noticing on a friend's lapel a button with the initials PBPWMGINFWMY. When I asked about it, the individual responded, "I know my life needs a great deal of improvement. But these initials remind me that God is conforming me to the image of Christ. They stand for: Please Be Patient With Me, God Is Not Finished With Me Yet!" The continuing assurance of that fact is the ongoing presence of Jesus in our lives, our belonging to Him, and His unconditional love for us.

When we think about Jesus, our precious and preeminent Lord, we are reminded that we are in Him and He is in us. God is conforming us to His image and therefore the hurtful words of others are really of little consequence!

Weapon #3: The Blood of Jesus

During a missions trip to Africa a young man experienced a few days of being under the weather. As he visited with local residents and described his symptoms, they could only guess at his malady. Ironically, each illness they suggested became one he assumed he had! Ultimately he settled on a dreary disease with foreboding long-range consequences. He was virtually useless during those few days overseas. His African disease occupied his every thought—until it was pointed out to him that his immunization record showed he had received an inoculation to prevent it. How sad!

When Jesus took our sin to the cross, He took it *all*—past, present, and future. There is no sin for which His blood did not atone— not one! For that reason no believer in Christ should be held captive by sinful words. All our (and others') transgressions, all our weaknesses, all our flaws are covered and defeated by the blood of the Lamb (Rev. 12:11). *We do not have a single problem for which the atonement does not have the answer!*

When the blood of Jesus was shed, He poured out His life so we could be redeemed. God "made Him who knew no sin to be sin for us, that we might become the righteousness of God in Him" (2 Cor. 5:21). Sadly, we often see the cross only in terms of its past accomplishment rather than in terms of its present effects. When the apostle Paul spoke about dying "daily" (1 Cor. 15:31) or being "crucified with Christ" (Gal. 2:20), he was referring to the *present activity of identifying with what Christ accomplished on the cross 2,000 years ago*. Because He gave His life for us then, we have access by prayer to God now, and what others have to say to or about us is, by comparison, insignificant.

A person who possesses a season ticket for a football team is not required to stand in line and purchase a ticket at each game. He simply shows his season ticket at the gate. The price has been paid, and he is thus entitled to the privileges of a ticket-holder.

Satan wants us to forget that the price has been paid for our life in Christ. Through the hurtful words of others, he often tries to persuade us to forget, and thus not use, the rights and privileges we possess as joint-heirs with Christ. He seeks to keep us from enjoying our position in the family of God. It is important to maintain an awareness of Jesus Christ's presence and rule in our lives, recognizing that we have been purchased with a price—His life. The Devil has no further claim on our lives, energies, or ambitions.

As my family and I prayed on that wonderful, life-changing evening I shared about earlier, we each broke the curse of words through *the Word of God, the character of Jesus*, and *the blood of Christ*. The experience brought spiritual revival to our hearts. It will do the same for all who come humbly and honestly before the Lord in prayer.

QUESTIONS FOR REFLECTION AND PRAYER

1. Does any curse of words exist in your life now—anything said by others that is holding you in bondage to fear or depression or a sense of inferiority or whatever? If so, how do those hurtful words stand up in light of the Word of God, the character of Christ, and the blood He shed for your redemption? Are those words consistent with who you are in Christ according to God's Word? Talk with God about this now.

2. Are hurtful words with which you are currently struggling consistent with the character of Christ into which you are being conformed? What can you do to allow God to do that work day by day?

What are you doing that in some way hinders this divine project? Pray about this right now.

3. Do the harmful words of others in your life reveal any sin or weakness with which you need to deal more fully? Be specific. What actions does God want you to take in regard to all this (confession, repentance, walking in newness of life, etc.)? Are you willing to take these steps? Why or why not? Discuss this with God now.

16

PRAYING THROUGH
YOUR SALVATION

Examine yourselves as to
whether you are in the faith.

2 CORINTHIANS 13:5

OVER THE YEARS I HAVE COUNSELED many faithful church members who in spite all of their dedicated Christian activity were keenly aware something was desperately wrong in their relationship with God. Many of these people have confessed to harboring years of nagging doubt about their salvation. Some have indicated they had slipped into the futile habit of daily asking the Lord to save them—"just in case I'm not already saved." A prayer like that is not born out of a deep conviction of sin, and it does not bring sweet assurance of salvation. Thus, it only adds confusion to an already troubled heart.

How should someone with a doubting heart pray about the most important issue of life—their relationship with God? When the apostle Paul challenged the Corinthians to "Examine yourselves as to whether you are in the faith. Test yourselves" (2 Cor. 13:5), he was insisting on an intense, personal examination of one's relationship with Christ. Again, in 1 Corinthians 11:28 ("But let a man examine himself"), Paul asked for the kind of evidence that can come only from testing.

It is both expedient and profitable to examine ourselves in regard to our salvation. But what questions should we prayerfully ask? And what evidences should be present? Romans 8:14-16 serves as a guide here.

> For as many as are led by the Spirit of God, these are sons of God. For you did not receive the spirit of bondage again to fear, but you received the Spirit of adoption by whom we cry out, "Abba, Father." The Spirit Himself bears witness with our spirit that we are children of God.

If we are struggling with doubts, we can prayerfully consider the following factors from Romans 8:14-16.

THE UPWARD PATH

Paul indicates that "sons of God" are "led by the Spirit of God" (Rom. 8:14). Beginning with the moment we can identify as the time of our conversion to Christ, we should see numerous evidences of God's leading us on an upward spiritual path. Are we continuing to grow closer to Him? Are we being conformed to the image of God's dear Son? This assures us that we belong to Him.

Some might question the necessity of such a consideration, claiming that it is unnecessary to recollect any beginning point in one's spiritual pilgrimage. Interestingly, the illustrations the Bible uses to denote the Christian life (marriage, adoption, birth) all have a significant point of beginning. It is difficult to imagine how a person who can remember other important encounters in life could have no recollection of passing from death to life! Granted, some do not remember the exact time or date of their salvation, but they nevertheless do recollect passing out of darkness into God's light.

The pilgrimage of our lives is marked by lapses, stumblings, moments of great failure and disappointment, battles with besetting sin—and by enlightenment, courage, victory over temptation, and increasing Christlikeness. Our life's journey resembles that of a mountain climber whose path consists of many ups and downs. Sometimes he takes a downward path because he has momentarily lost his way; he slips and falls occasionally as well. But regardless of his struggles and brief descents, the general direction of his path is toward the summit. Is an upward path a characteristic of our relationship with Christ? This is one encouraging evidence that we belong to Christ.

There is a common perception that *becoming* a Christian can be separated from *being* a Christian. But these are, in fact, inseparable. A person might think he is saved because he can remember "praying the prayer." But what about his life since then? Has he grown closer with the Lord or moved farther from Him? Would hearing him pray today be the same as hearing his prayers twenty years ago? Has his devotion to Christ deepened? Has his hatred of sin diminished or grown? Continuing upward progress is one evidence of genuine conversion.

Scripture clearly teaches that we are not saved by our good works (Eph. 2:8-9). But it also clearly states that people who are genuinely born again *will* give evidence of their salvation by the way they live. In other words, belief cannot be separated from behavior. In His Sermon on the Mount our Lord said, "Not everyone who says to Me, 'Lord, Lord,' shall enter the kingdom of heaven, but he who does the will of my Father in heaven" (Matt. 7:21). On another occasion He chided those who called Him Lord and yet did not do what He said (Luke 6:46). *True saving faith affects the way we conduct our lives.*

One of the most sobering statements in Scripture regarding the change that takes place when a person comes to believe in Christ is found in 1 John 3:6-9:

> *Whoever abides in Him does not sin. Whoever sins has neither seen Him nor known Him. Little children, let no one deceive you. He who practices righteousness is righteous, just as He is righteous. He who sins is of the devil; for the devil has sinned from the beginning. For this purpose the Son of God was manifested, that He might destroy the works of the devil. Whosoever is born of God does not sin, for His seed remains in him; and he cannot sin, because he has been born of God.*

In this passage "sin" implies "continual sin." So we could read the passage this way: "Whosoever abides in Him does not keep on committing the same old sins in the same old way with the same old feeling." For too long people have excused their spiritual deadness by including themselves in the group they call "the backslidden." But earlier in John's first letter the apostle points out that anyone who is habitually backslidden has probably never been genuinely born into God's family: "They went out from us, but they were not of us; for if they had been of us, they would have continued with us; but they went out that they might be made manifest, that none of them were of us" (2:19).

The fact that genuine salvation produces godly behavior is irrefutably stated in Hebrews 11. As we read there the "Roll Call of the Faithful," we discover that not one of those individuals was famous simply because of what he thought or how he felt. Each one was famous for the behavior that demonstrated his faith. Abel offered, Enoch walked, Noah prepared, Abraham went out, etc. In other words, though we are not saved by works, neither are we saved by the kind of faith that does not produce good works.

Some years ago I heard the chaplain of a Rotary Club pray, "Lord, be with these Rotarians today, for we know Thy way is the Rotary way." This man had reduced his expectations of the remarkable change that takes place at conversion to the point that it was no more demanding than the creed of a community service group. With all due respect to this misguided individual, meeting Jesus and passing from death to life, having old things pass away and all things become new, having our destination changed from an eternity in hell to an eternity in heaven, surrendering our lives to the One who is the Creator and the Sustainer of the universe and acknowledging Him as King of kings and Lord of lords will produce a life that is so radically different, no mere creed can embody it!

So the first certain sign of salvation is a life that continues on an upward path. If we have doubts about our salvation, we need to prayerfully go back to the time we consider to be the beginning of our Christian life. We can ask God to reveal evidences of genuine change and spiritual growth, or the lack of such, in our lives. Are we on an upward path?

AN OUTWARD PROFESSION

True believers eagerly testify that they know the Lord. Jesus said, "Therefore whoever confesses Me before men, him I will also confess before My Father who is in heaven. But whoever denies Me before men, him I will also deny before My Father who is in heaven" (Matt. 10:32-33). Genuine possession leads to joyful confession.

Paul indicated a similar criterion when he wrote to the believers in Rome, "For you did not receive the spirit of bondage again to fear, but you received the Spirit of adoption by whom we cry out, 'Abba, Father'" (8:15). "Abba," a word of tender endearment and communion, is more like our English word *daddy* than the more formal designation *father*. Paul is saying that the true believer, set free from bondage to sin and the law and having a new and intimate relationship as an adopted child of God, need feel no intimidation when coming to confessing the Lord.

Many people think personal matters, including salvation, must always be kept private. While faith is indeed a personal matter, it was never intended to be kept secret. My marriage ceremony was an intensely personal issue, but it was not private. The ring I wear on my finger is a constant visual reminder to everyone I meet that I belong to someone. Our Lord desires public confession!

The Lord is so interested in our outward profession that He even included it in the Great Commission He gave to us, in the ordinance of baptism. Baptism pictures death to an old way of life and rising to newness of life. This new life is then to be characterized by the same behavior expected of the first disciples—"teaching them to observe all things that I have commanded you" (Matt. 28:20). Every believer should be unashamed to say, show, and share his or her new life in Christ.

Many professing Christians have no sense of victory in their lives because of a stubborn refusal to allow an outward demonstration of their faith. I remember one prominent church leader who confessed that though baptized as a young man, he later became deeply convicted of his sin and his need of genuine salvation. In brokenness and repentance he received Christ by faith.

The next Sunday when the altar call was given in his local church, he started down the aisle to tell his pastor what had happened. But then he thought, *I'm a church leader. People will be disillusioned if they think I've been in a position of leadership all these years without really being saved. Making this decision would cause confusion, and I certainly don't want to do that. Anyway, salvation is a personal matter; what really matters is that I have trusted Christ.*

With tears this man confessed to me that through the years he had then become increasingly concerned about man's opinion rather than God's. He knew there would be no spiritual victory in his life until he made an outward profession of his faith. When he finally openly confessed his faith before his church family, many other men, in brokenness and with tears, came to the altar to receive Christ and follow Him in scriptural baptism.

The issue of course is greater than baptism. The point is that a believer must possess a growing eagerness to tell others about his relationship with Christ. The absence of such a desire probably evidences the absence of a genuine saving experience with Jesus Christ. Peter and John responded to those who threatened them, "For we cannot but speak the things which we have seen and heard" (Acts 4:20).

We should each ask ourselves if we are eager to be open witnesses to God's saving grace (Acts 1:8) and should ask God to reveal whether our regard for the opinion of men outweighs our eagerness to obey Him.

AN INWARD PEACE

When people ask me to help them pray through their doubts regarding salvation, I often encourage them to let God speak through the first epistle of John. The five brief chapters in that Bible book shed great light on how we can *know* we have salvation. In 4:13, for example, we are reminded, "By this we *know* that we abide in Him, and He in us, because He has given us of His Spirit." Similarly, Romans 8:16 reminds every believer that "The Spirit Himself bears witness with our spirit that we are children of God." This is perhaps the most convincing evidence of genuine salvation—the internal witness of God's Holy Spirit to our spirits.

Sometimes people who are in turmoil over the certainty of their salvation play intellectual games. *Let's see,* they think to themselves, *in Revelation 3:20 Jesus says He will come into my heart if I ask Him. I have asked Him, so He must be in my heart.* Unfortunately, this mind game never brings lasting peace, and soon the doubts return. *Am I really saved? Did I say the right words? Have I done the right things? Was I really sincere? Did I have enough faith?*

The simple truth contained in the 1 John passage quoted above is simply this: *The truly born-again person has a deep underlying sense of assurance that comes from the Spirit of God.* An experience, a decent life, church membership, and so on are good things in themselves; but having all your spiritual credentials properly aligned will bring no peace without the witness of God's Spirit confirming that you are indeed accepted in Christ.

While in college and dating my wife-to-be, I was perplexed to hear her say on more than one occasion, "Sometimes I wonder if I have eternal life." I just knew she must be a Christian. After all, she had made her "decision for Christ" in one of the largest churches in that state and had been baptized by one of the most noted pastors in the area. She had grown up in the church and had even surrendered to a "call to missions." On our first date we attended a Wednesday night worship service at which she led a missions group for young girls. Everything about her life indicated she was a Christian.

During the early years of our marriage, she again expressed doubts about her salvation. I attempted to resolve her misgivings through an appeal to her logic but failed. But God's Spirit prevailed! In the fifth year of our marriage she said, "You know, it really makes no difference what either of us says or thinks. I still do not possess inner peace! I am convinced I am lost!" She had lacked assurance because she had not truly come to know Christ as her Savior. She had not heard the witness of God's Spirit. That night she became a new creature in Christ!

It would be difficult for me to describe the change that then took place in her life. I thought she was already a perfect lady, but her transformed life became a challenge to me! Her insatiable hunger for the Word of God was incredible. She developed an earnest desire to see others come to Christ. Within hours of her conversion, she stood before the church, confessing her faith and following the Lord in believer's baptism. And through the years she has repeatedly remarked about the wonderful peace that the Spirit of God has brought to her heart.

A SAD STORY

Some years ago, after preaching a message on the evidences of salvation, I was confronted by an irritated church member who exclaimed, "You're just trying to sow doubt in the hearts of these fine church members. We are all right with God. We don't need to ask any questions about our faith!"

I sensed that beneath his anger was the fear that he had not experienced genuine conversion. But sadly, he refused to heed the scriptural admonition to examine himself (2 Cor. 13:5). Had he done so and found himself outside the faith, it would have been a simple matter to repent of sin and unbelief and turn to Christ for genuine salvation. And if he found himself to be a member of God's family, but weakened by sin, he would have been a candidate for a genuine, personal revival.

As the years passed, he became more hardened and embittered. Once an active church member, he now rarely attended, excusing his attitude with the complaint that there are so many hypocrites in the church. At his death, family members privately expressed to me their doubts about his conversion. Only God knows the truth, but his family could have been much comforted and blessed had he left a legacy of faith.

In the face of doubt we should go to our knees and talk candidly with the One who best understands us and who desires to give us full assurance of our salvation. Such an experience is both proper and probing, and it may prevent us from making life's most costly mistake.

QUESTIONS FOR REFLECTION AND PRAYER

1. Are you on an upward path? As you look back on your life since coming to know Christ, can you see how God has steadily

brought you closer to Himself and has led you into increasing godliness in your heart and life? In what ways? When this has not been your experience, why so? Are you currently progressing or regressing in your spiritual life? Pray to God about all this right now.

2. Are you making an outward profession? Do you find it easy or hard to openly confess that you belong to Christ? Why? With what effects on your life as a Christian? Do you generally live according to the old life or the new one? What can you do to consistently practice the latter? Discuss this with God now.

3. Do you have an inward peace? Are you confident that you are a member of God's family? Why or why not? How does the Holy Spirit assure you of this? What can you do to better hear the Spirit's voice to you on this matter? Why is this important? Talk this over with God now.

17

PRAYING THAT
CONQUERS TEMPTATION

. . . but with the temptation
will also make the way of escape.

1 CORINTHIANS 10:13

IT IS NOT AT ALL UNUSUAL for the serious student of prayer to face
severe temptation. Our Adversary, after all, is both corrupt in ambition and cunning in his strategy. This is why Peter reminds us to "be
sober, be vigilant, because your adversary the devil walks about like a
roaring lion, seeking whom he may devour" (1 Pet. 5:8). It is the
Enemy's evil desire to bring both discouragement and disillusionment
to anyone seeking effectiveness in prayer. It is wise, therefore, for us to
know how to deal adequately with temptation.

UNDERSTANDING THE NATURE OF TEMPTATION

It is important to consider both what temptation *is* and what it *is not*.
Temptation is an encouragement or an *inducement to sin*. From the
believer's standpoint, temptation is Satan's encouragement to be
merely human, to forget or reject both the *promises* of God for every
believer and the *privileges* that each believer possesses because of his
position in Christ. Satan would have the believer excuse sin with the
statement, "I'm only human."

The apostle Paul reminds us that excusing sin on the basis of our human nature is not an option open to the believer. "No temptation has overtaken you but such as is common to man; but God is faithful, who will not allow you to be tempted beyond what you are able, but with the temptation will also make the way of escape, that you may be able to bear it" (1 Cor. 10:13).

In other words, writes Paul, temptation is to be understood as a common and expected experience. But for the believer there is the assurance that the temptations you face will not exceed your capacity to respond properly. By His grace, God will provide a way of escape, thus giving you the power to endure the temptation. As a believer, you are not just human. Within you dwells the Lord Himself. By a supernatural experience of God's grace, old things have passed away, all things have become new. Your body is, in fact, the temple of the Holy Spirit.

While temptation is an inducement to sin, however, *it is not identical with sin*. In Luke 4:1–13 we read of our Lord's temptation in the wilderness. But though He was tempted in all points just like we are, He never committed sin (Hebrews 4:15).

Believers sometimes make the mistake of confusing temptation with sin. God does not judge mankind on the basis of temptation but, rather, on the reality of our sin. Perhaps Adam thought that God would be satisfied with his excuse for sin. "It was the woman," he alibied, "In fact," he said: "it was the woman *You* gave me!" Eve, in turn, responded with the age-old complaint that Satan was to blame for her sin. But God accepted none of these excuses. While we may be tempted by others, temptation and sin are not identical. We are held personally accountable for our sin, regardless of the source of temptation.

I mention this difference for the following reason: When you determine to be effective in prayer, you may immediately find yourself facing temptations of the most powerful sort. The tendency might be to shrug your spiritual shoulders and respond with a certain degree of resignation: "Oh well, I knew it was a hopeless pursuit anyway." Remember these two sides of temptation. Temptation is an inducement to sin, but it is not identical with sin. Be assured that there is a strategy by which you may gain victory over temptation.

CIRCUMSTANCES COMMON TO TEMPTATION

Satan's cleverness should never be underestimated. He is, indeed, a roaring lion, walking about and seeking whom he may devour. We should be aware that he stands ready to mount an attack at any time. Christ's example, however, indicates that there are certain times when we must be especially aware of our own vulnerability to temptation. Our Lord's experience of temptation recorded here, as well as in the other gospels, gives us a clear indication of the circumstances during which we often are tempted. In the following times you will find your-self particularly in need of standing guard against the wiles of the Devil.

When You Are Physically Weak

Jesus was tempted by Satan at the close of a forty-day period of fast-ing. This would have been a time of extreme physical weakness for Him. Is it not true that we are more open to temptation when we are physically weak? It is at the close of a long and arduous day, for instance, that discouragement may come, and with it, some bitter dis-agreement with those close to us.

This particular pre-condition to temptation may be the reason that sensual temptations often seem so powerful in the later hours of the evening when our defenses are down. I personally encourage cou-ples who are anticipating marriage to set limits on the time they spend together in the evenings as a way of dealing with this particularly dev-astating kind of temptation. Likewise, you would be wise to remain particularly vigilant when you are experiencing some type of physical weakness.

When You Are Preparing for a Great Spiritual Undertaking

Our Lord's time of fasting and prayer in the wilderness occurred at the very outset of His earthly ministry. By His baptism at the hands of John, He had been singled out as the Messiah. But prior to His very first Galilean tour the Lord now found Himself under the intense attack of Satan.

Many believers have experienced Satan's direct temptation as they prepared for a great spiritual ministry. Preachers tell me that distractions are at their worst as they are preparing their messages. Sunday school teachers have reminded me that it is when they settle down to prepare their Sunday school lesson that the phone seems to ring the most often or that the children need the most attention. How many of us have been witnessing to a nonbeliever only to face a great distraction at the most crucial moment of sharing?

It would be wise for anyone entering the arena of prayer to realize that the very nature of this pilgrimage invites satanic interference. If our Lord suffered such powerful temptation on the eve of His earthly ministry, certainly we should be alerted to the same possibility. Satan seeks to distract us at the beginning of crucial ministries. He does not have to worry that we will carry on if he can keep us from getting started in the first place.

After Enjoying a Great Spiritual Experience

This period of temptation in the life of our Lord occurred immediately following His baptism. "Jesus, being filled with the Holy Spirit, returned from the Jordan and was led by the Spirit into the wilderness" (Luke 4:1). What a high spiritual moment His baptism must have been! All three persons of the Trinity had manifested themselves. God the Son was baptized; God the Spirit, in the fashion of a dove, was hovering nearby; and God the Father spoke: "You are My beloved Son; in You I am well pleased." This was the moment of our Lord's introduction to the public as Messiah. What a moment!

Then, in a blatant attempt to take the edge off of the excitement, Satan came with his temptation. Is it not true in your own experience that some of your greatest temptations have occurred immediately following your highest moments of spiritual challenge or accomplishment? How many times have you heard someone say, "I don't know what's wrong with me. It seemed that God really spoke to my heart during our recent church revival, but now, just a few weeks later, I am so discouraged, depressed, and dejected. My spiritual life, which was at an all-time high, is now at an all-time low!" This is Satan's plan to cut our spiritual legs from under us. He would have us believe it was all nothing but emotion rather than spiritual reality.

It is intriguing to note how often our efforts to promote spiritual growth have inherent within them all three of these circumstances. When young people arrive home from camp, for instance, they have had a thrilling spiritual experience. They are preparing to change the world. They are physically exhausted. Walking into the house, they throw their bag of dirty clothes into a corner of their room and drop exhausted into bed. Mom walks by and asks, "How was camp?" Irritated, they roll over in bed and snort, "Don't bother me now." An argument ensues, and shortly it seems all that was gained has now been lost.

I am not at all suggesting that we can or should avoid such circumstances in our lives. They can be of inestimable value. But it is wise for us to be forewarned so that we may be especially vigilant.

SATAN'S TARGETS FOR TEMPTATION

When God created us, He gave us the remarkable capacity to live in two worlds at the same time. We were created as physical beings and given physical bodies so we could communicate with the physical world. But we are also spiritual beings. Genesis 1:27 tells us that we are created in the image of God. Again in John's Gospel, chapter 4, we are taught that God is a Spirit. Man was given a spiritual capacity so he could communicate with God, just as he was given a physical body with its five senses so he could communicate with the physical world.

Another aspect of man's personality is his soul. In the soul man processes the information that he receives, whether through his physical senses or by his spirit. And there, in his intellect and with his emotion he makes a decision of his will.

These three aspects of our personality (body, soul, and spirit) comprise the three arenas in which Satan seeks to tempt us, his targets. Notice how Satan attacked our Lord in these same three arenas.

When Physical Need Is Obvious

Satan said to the Lord, "If you are the Son of God, command this stone to become bread" (Luke 4:3). The Lord, you remember, was physically in need of nourishment. Here Satan was tempting Him to choose physical satisfaction over spiritual effectiveness. Satan was saying, "Your physical welfare is far more important than Your personal, spiritual integrity."

Prayer warriors often fight major battles in the arena of physical temptation. Such people generally make specific commitments regarding their personal, devotional lives. There is a strong desire to be more disciplined, to spend more time in prayer and in the study of God's Word. Often a choice has been made to rise early in the morning for the practice of prayer. But then the decision is put to the test. It will soon become evident whether physical comfort takes priority over spiritual effectiveness

Satan targets the arena of physical temptation more often than any other. The most common appeal of advertisers is to the sensual or physical. We are often told we "owe" ourselves certain physical pleasures. Our contemporary hedonistic society rationalizes, "You should indulge in whatever you enjoy, no matter the cost." This appeal to sensual satisfaction is as old as the Garden of Eden.

When Spiritual Compromise Appears Compelling

Luke records that Satan took Jesus to a high mountain. After showing Him all the kingdoms of the world, he stated, "All this authority I will give You, and their glory; for this has been delivered to me, and I give it to whomever I wish. Therefore, if You will worship before me, all will be Yours" (Luke 4:6–7).

What a temptation! Jesus had come to save those very people He had just seen in a moment of time. Satan, as "prince of this world," had gained this position of limited authority in the Garden. Now he was offering it to the Lord. All that was required was a perfunctory act of worship before Satan. Those for whom Jesus would die would be His . . . and without the agony of the Cross!

But Jesus saw straight through this ploy of Satan. The Devil was tempting Him to defile Himself with sin. It was as if Satan were hinting, "A little sin is appropriate in light of all You can accomplish." But Jesus knew that even the smallest sin would render it impossible for Him to redeem lost mankind even if He had authority over them.

How often Satan tempts us with spiritual compromise. "A little sin is acceptable for a big cause!" We are encouraged to tell "white lies" in order to "make people feel good about themselves." We are tempted to exaggerate our ministry reports or to use flattery to manipulate the decisions of others. "After all," we comment, "this is for the good of others."

How subtle is this temptation of Satan's. Is it actually possible that we can ever accomplish good by deliberately committing sin? I remember a man who claimed that in his particular business, he often had to violate small principles in order to achieve larger objectives. He boasted that this approach made it possible for him to give more dollars to the Lord's work. I reminded him that when a person is obeying God, he *never* needs to violate *any* principles.

When Soulish Effort Appears to Be a Shortcut to Success

Jesus was finally taken by Satan to Jerusalem, to "the pinnacle of the temple." "If You are the Son of God, throw Yourself down from here. For it is written: 'He shall give his angels charge over you, to keep you.' And, 'In their hands they shall bear you up, lest you dash your foot against a stone.'"

There is a sense in which the subtle appeal to the soul is the one to which we most often yield. Jesus knew that at that moment there was a priest standing in the temple looking toward the east. His responsibility was to scan the eastern sky for the appearance of the Messiah. What an impact it would have made for Jesus to float from the sky, borne up by a myriad of powerful angels! How impressive! In such a short time the world would come to sit at the feet of the Master in Jerusalem.

Here Satan's temptation was to do God's work, but to do it man's way. "Be the Messiah," he was saying, "But avoid all of the suffering; eliminate the necessity of faith. With one great, impressive event You can be heralded as the Savior of the World!" Notice the subtlety of this temptation. It is *not* the temptation to turn your back on the work of God, to become spiritually indifferent, or to deny God's purpose for your life. "Oh no," argues Satan, "Do the work of God, but *do it your way.*"

God's work done our way will not receive His supply. He is only committed to supporting what He initiates. Do it your way and there will come a time when you have gone as far as your own natural gifts and abilities will carry you.

Jacob's experience gives us a perfect illustration of this truth. Remember that moment at the brook of Jabbok when he pulled the last trick out of his bag and found that he could continue in his cleverness no longer? It was then that he realized the necessity of doing God's work in God's way. There he received his new name, Israel, as an indication of his new nature—one who had power with God.

Looking carefully at your life, can you identify Satan's temptations in these three arenas—body, soul, and spirit? Can you identify the arena in which you find yourself most often experiencing failure before Satan's clever inducements? You have determined to become mighty in prayer. The result is that Satan has now declared an all-out war against you in these three arenas. But, dear friend, there is a road to victory.

A STRATEGY FOR VICTORY

We are not left powerless when we face temptation. Remember Paul's words to every believer: "God is faithful, who will not allow you to be tempted beyond what you are able, but with the temptation will make the way of escape" (1 Cor. 10:13). Our strategy for victory is identical to that employed by the Lord. From the gospel record we may outline a plan by which we can successfully defeat Satan in these arenas of temptation. Here is how to "pray through" when tempted.

Remember Your Position

Jesus responded to Satan's temptation with the words, "You shall not tempt the LORD your God" (Luke 4:12). This was His reminder to Satan that He was positioned as part of the divine Godhead, a member of the Trinity. To tempt the Lord was in effect to tempt God Himself.

As a believer, you are part of the body of Christ. When you pray in the name of Jesus, you are reminding both yourself and Satan that for Satan to tempt you is for him to incur the attention of God and to invite His power and wrath. When you remind Satan of the blood of Jesus, you are stating quite forcefully that is the blood that has bought you. Christ's blood represents His finished work on the cross; His death as payment for our sin brought total defeat to Satan.

Rest on the Promises

Note how our Lord quoted Scripture to Satan. "It is written . . ." emphasized Jesus. It is crucial to remember that Satan is not bound by our imagination or thoughts, no matter how holy they may seem. But God's Word is absolutely binding upon him. In essence, through the use of God's Word we are exercising our "power of attorney" against Satan.

God's Word is absolutely true. The psalmist said, "Forever, O Lord, Your word is settled in heaven" (Ps. 119:89). In other words, it is an established fact. This is why it is so vital to rest on the promises of God when dealing with Satan's temptations.

Resist the Adversary as a Person

"Be sober, be vigilant; because your adversary the devil walks about like a roaring lion, seeking whom he may devour. Resist him, steadfast in the faith" (1 Pet. 5:8–9).

Many people fail in the area of dealing with temptation because they do not understand the nature of the battle. They try to overcome the temptation itself rather than to resist the one who is bringing that temptation to them. Paul reminds us that "we wrestle not against flesh and blood, but against *principalities*, against *powers*, against the *ruler* of the darkness of this age, against *spiritual hosts* of wickedness [wicked spirits] in the heavenly places" (Eph. 6:12)

Have you ever thought of the folly of trying to stop thinking about something? In reality, the harder you try not to think of it, the more you actually think about it. Similarly, we will struggle with our temptations until we direct the forces of God upon the Tempter rather than being occupied with it in our own minds. We must resist the person of Satan through God's power.

Be Ready with a Pronouncement

A final aspect of resisting Satan and thus of overcoming temptation is that of making an actual, verbal pronouncement. We must remember here that Satan is *not* omniscient. He cannot read your thoughts. Jesus did not simply direct His thoughts toward Satan, thus causing him to flee. Rather, the Scripture specifically states that He *spoke* to the Adversary.

How effective it is when we employ this particular aspect of our strategy! When we come against the Adversary in the name of Jesus, because we are His blood-bought children, and when we resist him by employing the actual Word of God, the promises of Scripture, we will find it far easier to deal with temptation by overcoming the Tempter.

It is important for a believer to fill his heart with the Word of God. Doing so is the equivalent of stocking your spiritual ammunition belt with artillery, deadly in its effect, to throw against Satan as he and his emissaries throw temptation at you. Perhaps this is why the psalmist reminds us, "How can a young man cleanse his way? By taking heed according to Your word" (Ps. 119:9). And again, "Your word have I hidden in my heart, that I might not sin against You" (Ps. 119:11). And again, "I have restrained my feet from every evil way, that I might keep Your word" (Psalm 119:101).

WHAT TO EXPECT

It is helpful to understand not only the nature of the battle and the strategy to be used in dealing with temptation, but *when* that strategy is to be employed. Once again we are instructed by the Lord's experience.

We are impressed with the initial victory over temptation. After Jesus employed Scripture in His rebuke for the third time, the Devil ended the temptation (Luke 4:13). Employment of the strategy mentioned above will lead you into a pitched battle against the Adversary. The continued use of this strategy will ultimately result in victory. We are reminded that when we "resist the devil . . . he will flee from you" (James 4:7). There is nothing quite so exhilarating as seeing your enemy flee in the face of a barrage of Scripture hurled in Jesus' name from your position, under His blood.

But we are also told that the devil departed from Jesus "until an opportune time" (Luke 4:13). It is plain that Satan constantly dogged the path of our Lord right up to the very moment when He was hanging on the cross. Unfortunately, some are under the impression that some great event in their Christian life will once and for all make them impervious to temptation. They anticipate that such an event will eliminate the necessity of ever doing battle again with the Adversary. They expect that their fleshly spirit will be so controlled as never to give difficulty again.

If this is the case, we are then left with the strange and seemingly unnecessary references throughout Scripture to the fact that believers are to be vigilant warriors dressed in full armor and ready to employ the arsenal of weapons God has given them to use against the forces of Satan. We should be reminded once again that the servant is not greater than his Lord. Since temptation was a frequent occurrence during Jesus' earthly ministry, should we expect anything less?

It should come as encouragement to each of us that Canaan was just as filled with battles as was the wilderness. The one notable difference is that in the wilderness we often find God's people fighting *against* Him. But in Canaan we see them fighting *with* God *against* the Adversary. Entering the arena of prayer does not remove you from battle, but it does insure that you are fighting *with* Him *against* the forces of Satan. From that vantage point, you are capable of overcoming temptation and going forward with God.

QUESTIONS FOR REFLECTION AND PRAYER

1. Does Jesus' example of being tempted by the Devil at a time of physical need, at the beginning of a dynamic spiritual ministry, offer any help for you in your situations of temptation? Why or why not? If so, in what way? Talk to Jesus about your most difficult current temptations.

2. Can you identify Satan's temptations regarding your body, soul, and spirit? Can you identify the area in which you find yourself most often experiencing failure regarding Satan's clever enticements? In what ways is the Devil trying to get you to compromise? What would be the results? What can you do to avoid falling to these temptations? Pray about this right now.

3.   Remembering your position—resting on God's promises—
resisting the Adversary—replying with a pronouncement—are you
taking these steps to victory in your life? Why or why not? How would
your life be different if you were more consistent in these areas?
Discuss this with God now.

18

Praying for Genuine Revival

*"If My people who are called by My name
will humble themselves, and pray and seek My face, and turn
from their wicked ways, then I will hear from heaven, and
will forgive their sin and heal their land."*

2 Chronicles 7:14

WHAT STARTED OUT AS THE "ANNUAL REVIVAL" on a Southern Baptist theological seminary campus became genuine revival when God took over the first chapel service. In the days that followed, the Holy Spirit brought deep conviction of sin to both students and faculty. Students confessed to their professors that they had not been totally honest on reading assignments and tests. Professors confessed to professional jealousy and competitiveness. In response to an awesome wave of God's power, all were moved first to confession and then to repentance. In the end, God brought wonderful restoration, affecting first the atmosphere of the campus, then spilling over into the homes and churches of students and faculty.

At the heart of genuine revival is repentance. Prayers of confession are harbingers of changed attitudes and lives. We readily acknowledge the necessity of repentance (turning away from sin) in salvation. But remember, our salvation is to be the pattern for the balance of our Christian life as well. "As you therefore have received Christ Jesus the

Lord, so walk in Him" (Col. 2:6). Since repentant confession was fundamental to our salvation experience, it must also play an important part in our daily walk with Christ.

Every true child of God can rejoice in the eternal security of his or her relationship with Him. But sin drives a wedge in our fellowship with God. Therefore, all disobedience must be prayerfully confessed and rejected if the intimacy of that fellowship is to be maintained.

THE REALITY OF SIN IN THE BELIEVER'S LIFE

The Bible is clear on the fact that God's people are not immune to sin. Our struggle with wickedness is real, and the Bible pictures us as combatants in the arena of faith. Consider the lives of past great men of God. Noah's faith qualified him to be the one man enlisted to provide a remnant after the Flood; yet he fell into sin after that great deliverance. Abraham, the great man of faith, was not untouched by sin; in fact, his ill-fated journey to Egypt produced a relationship out of which was born a nation that continually opposed God's people. Moses, the heroic and faithful leader of the Israelites, brought them to the border of the Promised Land but was not permitted to enter in himself because of his sin. And David, the man after God's own heart, had a secret sin that has been known around the world for over 2,000 years.

Listen to the heart-rending lament of the apostle Paul. He was obviously no stranger to sin either.

> For I know that in me (that is, in my flesh) nothing good dwells;
> for to will is present with me, but how to perform what is good
> I do not find. For the good that I will to do, I do not do; but
> the evil I will not to do, that I practice. Now if I do what I will
> not to do, it is no longer I who do it, but sin that dwells in me.
> I find then a law, that evil is present with me, the one who wills
> to do good. For I delight in the law of God according to the
> inward man. But I see another law in my members, warring
> against the law of my mind, and bringing me into captivity to
> the law of sin which is in my members. O wretched man that
> I am! Who will deliver me from this body of death? I thank

God—through Jesus Christ our Lord! So then, with the mind
I myself serve the law of God, but with the flesh the law of sin.
                                   —ROMANS 7:18-25

The first epistle of John also portrays the reality of sin in the
believer's life:

> *If we say that we have no sin, we deceive ourselves, and the*
> *truth is not in us. If we confess our sins, He is faithful and just*
> *to forgive us our sins and to cleanse us from all unrighteous-*
> *ness. If we say that we have not sinned, we make Him a liar,*
> *and His word is not in us. My little children, these things I write*
> *to you, so that you may not sin. And if anyone sins, we have*
> *an Advocate with the Father, Jesus Christ the righteous. And*
> *He Himself is the propitiation for our sins, and not for ours*
> *only but also for the whole world.*
>   —1 JOHN 1:8—2:2

The point is obvious: believers struggle with the reality of sin.
Intimate fellowship with God will only be maintained as we acknowledge any sin that has disturbed and diminished the quality of our relationship with Him.

THE REPULSIVENESS OF SIN IN THE BELIEVER'S LIFE

God insists that restoration of fellowship is directly related to our willingness to see the wickedness of our sin, to see our disobedience as He
sees it (2 Chron. 7:14; 1 John 1:8, 10). Sin is disgusting to God.
Though He shows grace to repentant sinners, He cannot look upon
sin itself with the least degree of tolerance. "But the wicked are like the
troubled sea, when it cannot rest, whose waters cast up mire and dirt.
'There is no peace,' says my God, 'for the wicked'" (Isa. 57:20-21).
While the sin of the lost world is repulsive to God, the sins of His people are even more so! If we confess, He forgives and cleanses; but if we
refuse to admit our transgression, He will not restore the fellowship
we have so foolishly broken.

Imagine, for instance, a man who after a beautiful time of

courtship finally rejoices in the privilege of taking his beloved as his wife. She becomes the focus of his love, the object of his affection. He lives for her and sacrifices all for her. When he is away from her, his thoughts are still upon the great joy it is to have her as his wife. She is on his mind and heart night and day. He always carries her picture with him and proudly tells others how blessed he is to have her as his wife. He would bend heaven and earth to fulfill her every request. She is the great love of his life.

But what this faithful and dedicated man does not know is that secretly, through the years of their courtship and now their marriage, she is a practicing prostitute. During the day, while he is at work and dreaming of her, she is in one adulterous bed after another. Though he remains faithful to her, she has lost count of her lovers. Imagine the heartbreak when he discovers the truth.

The true Church, all who have truly received Christ as Savior, is the bride of Christ. He died for her, and now He lives for her. His heart's great desire is that she may be presented one day before the Father pure and holy in her radiant, righteous apparel. But she is sometimes a prostitute, and God knows it. Her sinful flirtations and outright adulteries with the world pierce His heart moment by moment and will continue to do so until one day He calls His bride home to heaven. We, members of that Church, redeemed but sometimes unfaithful, have played the harlot with the lover of our souls. How repulsive our sin must be to our Savior! How we must wound His heart who shed his life's blood to cleanse us from the moral corruption we had chosen!

The brokenness that attends personal, spiritual revival comes when God's people begin to see their disobedience as God sees it and to acknowledge its awfulness. Historically, in the early days of great revival movements, there was not so much the song of joy as weeping prayers of repentance. Believers on the verge of spiritual awakening are usually found on their faces, crying out before the Lord about the repulsiveness of sin in their lives. They have a fresh appreciation for the fact that believers must not continue in widespread wickedness because they have been born of God (see 1 John 3:6-9).

GOD'S RESPONSE TO SIN IN THE BELIEVER'S LIFE

The Scriptures indicate that God deals with sin in believers' lives through a series of three progressive and increasingly drastic steps: conviction, chastening, and, finally, the call home ("sin leading to death," 1 John 5:16).

God's first response to our sin is to bring *conviction* to our hearts. To do this, the Holy Spirit employs the Word of God, which is "living and powerful, and sharper than any two-edged sword, piercing even to the division of soul and spirit, and of joints and marrow, and is a discerner of the thoughts and intents of the heart" (Heb. 4:12). God speaks to us through His Word about the sin in our lives. Just as a mirror reveals how we look to others, the Word of God reveals how we look to Him. The Holy Spirit uses the Word much like a sailor uses a compass, showing us where we have strayed from the course He has charted for our lives.

But suppose we make no course correction? What if we ignore the Spirit's voice and do not confess and repent of our sin? God then begins the process of *chastisement*.

> *And you have forgotten the exhortation which speaks to you as to sons: "My son, do not despise the chastening of the LORD, nor be discouraged when you are rebuked by Him; for whom the LORD loves He chastens, and scourges every son whom He receives." If you endure chastening, God deals with you as with sons; for what son is there whom the Father does not chasten? But if you are without chastening, of which all have become partakers, then you are illegitimate and not sons. Furthermore, we have had human fathers who corrected us, and we paid them respect. Shall we not much more readily be in subjection to the Father of spirits and live? For they indeed for a few days chastened us as seemed best to them, but He for our profit, that we may be partakers of His holiness. Now no chastening seems to be joyful for the present, but painful; nevertheless, afterward it yields the peaceable fruit of righteousness to those who have been trained by it.*
>
> —HEBREWS 12:5-11

Scripture plainly teaches that chastening (God's response to persistent sin) is so common for a believer that the failure to experience it
indicates that an individual is not actually a child of God.

But what happens if God's child does not respond to either conviction or chastisement? God might then possibly *call the believer
home.* First John 5:16 speaks about "sin leading to death." This probably refers not so much to a specific sin but to a specific *attitude*
toward sin—the deliberate choice to persist in sin in spite of God's
attempts to bring an about-face. Such a person is so confident of his
relationship with the Father (or takes it so lightly) that he is willing to
presume upon His love by stubbornly engaging in what is so repulsive
to Him. If a believer continues to ignore God's voice and chastisement,
he might well reap the judgment of Luke 13:9, "And if it bears fruit,
well. But if not, after that you can cut it down."

We must all beware of falling prey to sin, whether overt or more
subtle. David saw presumptuous sin as a most serious matter. Listen to
his plea: "Keep back Your servant also from presumptuous sins; let them
not have dominion over me. Then I shall be blameless, and I shall be
innocent of great transgression" (Ps. 19:13). We should remember that
although David occasionally sinned greatly, when he was confronted by
the prophet of God, his heart melted, and his spirit was broken.

God has committed Himself to deal with all sin in the believer's life.
He may do it through conviction, chastening, or death. But above all,
He wants us to turn away from sin so we can return to Him, come back
to His table, and enjoy restored fellowship. Like the prodigal son, fellowship with our Father awaits us at the end of the road of repentance.

RESTORATION FOR THE BELIEVER WHO SINS

God's familiar promise to Israel is one that we can claim as well: "If My
people who are called by My name will humble themselves, and pray and
seek My face, and turn from their wicked ways, then I will hear from
heaven, and will forgive their sin and heal their land" (2 Chron. 7:14).

It is remarkable that in spite of our sin, God desires to keep the
way open for fellowship with Him. This is irrefutable evidence of His
long-suffering grace.

This promise of restoration is preceded by six conditions:

- Salvation ("if My people").
- External evidence through Christlike behavior ("who are called by My name").
- Genuine humility ("will humble themselves").
- Earnest prayer ("and pray").
- An intense search for the heart of God ("and seek My face").
- Repentance ("and turn from their wicked ways").

These conditions in no way diminish the fact that restoration is ultimately a sovereign work of God, not something He is obligated to do because of some sort of merit in us apart from the work of Christ. God moves toward those whose lives exhibit these characteristics simply because He chooses to do so.

A coach can put any team member he chooses into the game; but in making that choice, he will be predisposed to use those players who have diligently conditioned themselves for competition. Similarly, if we desire to walk in fellowship with the sovereign God of heaven, we should earnestly pursue the conditions presented in 2 Chronicles 7:14.

Note carefully the character of this restoration. It is threefold. God first states that *He will hear the pleas of our heart*. Since we know that God has repeatedly told us He wants our fellowship, we can trust that it is His will for us and claim the following promise: "Now this is the confidence that we have in Him, that if we ask anything according to His will, He hears us. And if we know that He hears us, whatever we ask, we know that we have the petitions that we have asked of Him" (1 John 5:14-15).

Second, *God will forgive our sins*. "If we confess our sins, He is faithful and just to forgive us our sins and to cleanse us from all unrighteousness" (1 John 1:9). This is not a forgiveness for salvation. The subjects of this passage are children of God. This forgiveness and cleansing are necessary for the day-by-day maintenance of intimate communion with God.

Finally, *God promises to heal our land*. Many times when we talk about the sickness of our nation, we are in reality only speaking of the symptoms or evidences of sin. But when the Lord heals our land, He moves straight to the cause of those symptoms by bringing cleansing and restored fellowship. Speaking to sinful Israel, God urged, "'Come now, and let us reason together,' says the LORD, 'though your sins are like scarlet, they shall be as white as snow; though they are red like crimson, they shall be as wool. If you are willing and obedient, you shall eat the good of the land; but if you refuse and rebel, you shall be devoured by the sword'; for the mouth of the LORD has spoken" (Isa. 1:18-20).

A CLOSING WORD

God calls us away from our sin and back to restored fellowship. Following the promise of restoration (2 Chron. 7:14), the Lord says, "Now My eyes will be open and My ears attentive to prayer made in this place" (2 Chron. 7:15). In essence, God is saying, "Here are the *conditions* of restoration. Here is the *character* of that restoration. Now I am *calling* you to restoration. I am watching for your repentance; I am listening for your prayer. The next move is yours."

A friend has said to me on more than one occasion, "If God is silent, it's your move! The ball is in your court." If besetting sins have disrupted our fellowship with God, we must hurry to the place of prayer. Our eager confession will be met by God's forgiveness—and fellowship will be restored!

QUESTIONS FOR REFLECTION AND PRAYER

1. Are you generally enjoying unbroken fellowship with God? Why or why not? Do you find it easy or difficult to see the sin in your life the way God sees it? Do you rationalize or acknowledge your proneness to wander? Why? Talk this over with God now.

2. How do you generally respond to God's conviction or chastening regarding sin in your life? Why? With what results? Do you really believe God chastens you because He loves you? When you turn back to Him, is He waiting with open arms, like the father of the prodigal son? Discuss this with God now.

3. Have you experienced God's restoring power in your life? Do you need to seek that now? Which of the six conditions in 2 Chronicles 7:14 do you most need to obey today? Pray to God about this right now.

An Encouraging Voice
From the Past

"And whatever you ask in My name,
that I will do, that the Father may be glorified in the Son
If you ask anything in My name, I will do it."

JOHN 14:13-14

DURING THE EARLY YEARS OF THIS CENTURY, the Lisu tribespeople in southwest China experienced a remarkable movement of God. Many among the thousands who came to Christ were borne into the presence of God by the prayers and work of Mr. J. O. Fraser, a missionary of the Overseas Missionary Fellowship, formerly called the China Inland Mission. Mr. Fraser, like J. Hudson Taylor before him, saw that the success of his missionary work rested on the prayer support of those back home in England. In a letter written to encourage their continued prayers, he suggested that the "prayer of faith" follows certain guidelines. The letter, quoted here, emphasizes and amplifies the principles we have considered in this book.

TANTSAH, YUNNAN, CHINA
OCTOBER 9, 1915

MY DEAR FRIENDS:
The Scriptures speak of several kinds of prayer. There is intercession and there is supplication; there is labor in prayer and there is the

prayer of faith; all perhaps the same fundamentally, but they present various aspects of this great and wonderful theme. It would not be unprofitable to study the differences between these various scriptural terms.

There is a distinction between *general* prayer and *definite* prayer. By definite prayer I mean prayer after the pattern of Matthew 21:21-22 and John 15:7, where a definite petition is offered up and definite faith exercised for its fulfillment. Now faith must be in exercise in the other kind of prayer also, when we pray for many and varied things without knowing the will of God in every case.

In *general prayer* I am limited by my ignorance. But this kind of prayer is the duty of us all (I Tim. 2:1-2), however vague it has to be. I may know very little, in detail, about the object of my prayer, but I can at any rate commend it to God and leave it all with Him. It is good and right to pray, vaguely, for all people, all lands, all things, at all times. But *definite prayer* is a very different matter. It is in a special sense "the prayer of faith." A definite request is made in definite faith for a definite answer.

Take the case of a Canadian immigrant as an illustration of the prayer of faith. Allured by the prospect of "golden grain" he leaves home for the Canadian West. He has a definite object in view. He knows very well what he is going for, and that is wheat. He thinks of the good crops he will reap and of the money they will bring him—much like the child of God who sets out to pray the prayer of faith. He has his definite object too. It may be the conversion of a son or daughter; it may be power in Christian service; it may be guidance in a perplexing situation, or a hundred and one other things—but it is definite. Consider the points of resemblance between the cases of the prospective Canadian farmer and the believing Christian:

1. *The breadth of the territory*. Think of the unlimited scope for the farmer in Canada. There are literally millions of acres waiting to be cultivated. No need, there, to tread on other people's toes! Room for all—vast tracts of unoccupied land just going to waste, and good land too. And so it is with us, surely. There is a vast, vast field for us to go up and claim in faith. There is enough sin, enough sorrow, enough of the blighting influence of Satan in the world to absorb all

our prayers of faith, and a hundred times as many more. "There remaineth yet very much land to be possessed."

2. *The government encourages immigration.* Think also of the efforts of the Canadian government to encourage immigration. All the unoccupied land belongs to it, but settlers are so badly needed that they are offered every inducement—immigration office established, sea passages and railway fares reduced, and grants of land made free! And God is no less urgently inviting His people to pray the prayer of faith: "*Ask—ask—ask,*" He is continually saying to us. He offers His inducement too: "Ask, and ye shall receive, that your joy may be full." All the unoccupied territory of faith belongs to Him. And he bids us to come and occupy freely. "How long are ye slack to go in to possess the land?"

3. *There are fixed limits.* Yet this aspect of the truth must not be overemphasized. Blessed fact though it be that the land is so broad, it can easily be magnified out of due proportion. The important thing is not the vastness of the territory but how much of it is actually assigned to us. The Canadian government will make a grant of 160 acres to the farmer-immigrant, and no more. Why no more? Because they know very well he cannot work any more. If they were to give him 160 square miles instead of 160 acres he would not know what to do with it all. So they wisely limit him to an amount of land equal to his resources.

And it is much the same with us when praying the prayer of definite faith. The very word "definite" means "with fixed limits." We are often exhorted, and with reason, to ask great things of God. Yet there is a balance in all things, and we may go too far in this direction. It is possible to bite off, in prayer, more than we can chew. There is a principle underlying II Corinthians 10:13 which may apply to this very matter: "According to the measure of the province [limit] which God apportioned to us as a measure" (A.S.V.). Faith is like muscle, which grows stronger and stronger with use, rather than rubber, which weakens when it is stretched. Overstrained faith is not pure faith; there is a mixture of the carnal element in it. There is no strain in the "rest of faith." It asks for definite blessing as God may lead. It does not hold back through carnal timidity, nor press ahead too far through carnal eagerness.

I have definitely asked the Lord for several hundred families of Lisu believers. There are upward of two thousand Lisu families in the Tantsah district. It might be said, "Why do you not ask for a thousand?" I answer quite frankly, "Because I have not faith for a thousand." I believe the Lord has given me faith for more than one hundred families, but not for a thousand. So I accept the limits the Lord, I believe, has given me. Perhaps God will give me a thousand; perhaps He will lead me to commit myself to this definite prayer of faith later on. This is in accordance with Ephesians 3:20: "above all that we ask or think." But we must not overload faith; we must be sane and practical. Let us not claim too little in faith, but let us not claim too much either. Remember the Canadian immigrant's 160 acres. Consider, too, how the Dominion Government exercises authority in the matter of location. The government has a say as to the *where* as well as the *how much* of the immigrant's claim. He is not invited to wander all over the prairie at his own sweet will and elect to settle down in any place he chooses. Even in regard to the position of his farm he must consult the government.

Do we always do this in our prayers and claims? Do we consult the heavenly government at the outset, or do we pray the first thing that comes to mind? Do we spend time waiting upon God to know His will before attempting to embark on His promises? That this is a principle upon which God works He has informed us very plainly in I John 5:14-15. I cannot but feel that this is one cause for many unanswered prayers. James 4:3 has a broad application, and we need to search our hearts in its light. Unanswered prayers have taught me to seek the Lord's will instead of my own. I suppose most of us have had such experiences. We have prayed and prayed and prayed, and no answer has come. The heavens above us have been as brass. Yea, blessed brass, if it has taught us to sink a little more of this ever-present self of ours into the cross of Christ. Sometimes our petition has been such a good one, to all appearance, but that does not insure its being of God. Many "good desires" proceed from our uncrucified selves. Scripture and experience agree that those who live nearest to

God are the most likely to know His will. We are called to be "filled with the knowledge of His will" (Col. 1:9). We need to know more of the fellowship of Christ's death. We need to feed on the Word of God more than we do. We need more holiness, more prayer. We shall not, then, be in such danger of mistaking His will.

The wonderful promise of John 15:7 is prefixed by a far-reaching "if." I wonder if that verse might not be paraphrased: "If ye abide *not* in me, and my words abide *not* in you, *do not* ask whatsoever ye will, for it shall *not* be done unto you." Perhaps if we examined ourselves more thoroughly before God we might even discover, in some cases, that the whole course of our life was not in accordance with His will. What right would a man have, in such a case, to expect his prayers to be answered? But is not this the fact with regard to much "good" Christian work? "Get your work from God" is a good injunction. How often Christian leaders make their own plans, work hard at them, and then earnestly seek God's blessing on them. How much better, as Hudson Taylor felt, to wait on God to know His plans before commencing! Much Christian work seems to have the stamp of the carnal upon it. It may be "good," it may be successful outwardly, but the Shekinah glory is not there. Now all this applies to the prayer of faith. We must have the assurance that we are in the right place, doing the right work. We must be sure that God is leading us, when we enter upon specific prayer. It does not follow that because a thing is the will of God, He will necessarily lead *you* to pray for it. He may have other burdens for you. We must *get our prayers from God*, and pray to know His will. It may take time. God was dealing with Hudson Taylor for fifteen years before he laid upon him the burden of definite prayer for the foundation of the China Inland Mission. God is not in a hurry. He cannot do things with us until we are trained and ready for them. We may be certain He has further service, further burdens of faith and prayer to give us when we are ready for them.

4. *The claim endorsed*. Turn to the immigrant again. He has come to an agreement with the Canadian government. He falls in with their terms, he accepts their conditions, he agrees to take over the land allotted to him. So he presents his claim at the proper quarter, and it is at once endorsed. Could anything be more simple? Nor need our claim

in the presence of God be any less simple. When we once have the deep, calm assurance of His will in the matter, we put in our claim just as a child before his father. A simple request and nothing more. No cringing, no beseeching, no tears, no wrestling. No second asking either.

In my case I prayed continually for the Tengyueh Lisu for over four years, asking many times that several hundred families might be turned to God. This was only general prayer, however. God was dealing with me in the meantime. You know how a child is sometimes rebuked by his parents for asking something in a wrong way—perhaps asking rudely. The parent will respond, "Ask me properly!" That is just what God seemed to be saying to me then. "Ask Me properly! You have been asking Me to do this for the last four years without ever really believing I would do it—now ask *in faith*."

I felt the burden *clearly*. I went to my room alone one afternoon and knelt in prayer. I knew that the time had come for the prayer of faith. And then, fully knowing what I was doing and what it might cost me, I definitely committed myself to this petition *in faith*. I cast my burden upon the Lord and rose from my knees with the deep, restful conviction that I had already received the answer. The transaction was done. And since then (nearly a year ago now) I have never had anything but peace and joy (when in touch with God) in holding to the ground already claimed and taken. I have never repeated the request and never will: there is no need. The asking, the taking, and the receiving occupy but a few moments (Mark 11:24). It is a solemn thing to enter into a faith covenant with God. It is binding on both parties. You lift up your hand to God, you definitely ask for and definitely receive His proffered gift—then do not go back on your faith, even if you live to be a hundred.

5. *Get to work*. To return once more to the Canadian farmer, he has put in his claim, the land has been granted, the deed made out and sealed with the official seal. Is that the end then? No, only the beginning!

He has not yet attained his objective. His objective is a harvest of wheat, not a patch of wasteland, and there is a vast difference between the two. The government never promised him sacks of flour all ready for export—only the land which could be made to yield them. Now is the time for him to roll up his sleeves and get to work. He must build his homestead, get his livestock, call in laborers, clear the ground, plow it and sow his seed. The government says to him in effect, "We have granted your claim—now go and work it!"

And this distinction is no less clear in the spiritual realm. God gives us the ground in answer to the prayer of faith, but not the harvest. That must be worked for in cooperation with Him. Faith must be followed up by works, prayer-works. Salvation is of grace, but it must be worked out (Phil. 2:12) if it is to become ours. And the prayer of faith is just the same. It is given to us by free grace, but it will never be ours until we follow it up, work it out. Faith and works must never be divorced, for indolence will reap no harvest in the spiritual world. I think the principle will be found to hold in any case where the prayer of faith is offered, but there is no doubt that it always holds good in cases where the strongholds of Satan are attacked, where the prey is to be wrestled from the strong.

Think of the children of Israel under Joshua. God had given them the land of Canaan—given it to them, notice, by free grace—but see how they had to fight when once they commenced actually to take possession!

Satan's tactics seem to be as follows: He will first of all oppose our breaking through to the place of a real, living faith by all means in his power. He detests the prayer of faith, for it is an authoritative "notice to quit." He does not so much mind rambling, carnal prayers, for they do not hurt him much. This is why it is so difficult to attain to a definite faith in God for a definite object. We have often to strive and wrestle in prayer (Eph. 6:10-12) before we attain this quiet, restful faith. And until we break right through and *join hands with God* we have not attained to real faith at all. Faith is a gift of God—if we stop short of it we are using mere fleshly energy or will power, weapons of no value in this warfare. Once we attain to real faith, however, all the forces of hell are impotent to annul it. What then? They retire and muster their forces on this plot of ground which God has pledged Himself to give us, and contest every inch of it. The real battle begins when the prayer of faith has been offered. But, praise God, we are on the winning side! Let us read and reread Joshua 10 and never talk about defeat again. Defeat, indeed! No. Victory! Victory! Victory!

Please read 2 Samuel 23:8-23. All I have been saying is found in a nutshell in verses 11 and 12. Let Shammah represent the Christian warrior. Let David represent the crucified and risen Christ—and note that Shammah was "one of the mighty men that David had." Let the "plot of ground" represent the prayer of faith. Let the lentils, if you will, represent the poor lost souls of men. Let the Philistines represent the hosts of wickedness. Let "the people" represent Christians afflicted with spiritual anemia.

I can imagine what these people were saying as they saw the Philistines approaching and ran away. "Perhaps it was not the Lord's will to grant us that plot of ground. We must submit to the will of God."

Yes, we must indeed submit ourselves to God, but we must also "resist the devil" (James 4:7). The fact that the enemy comes upon us in force is no proof that we are out of the line of God's will. The constant prefixing of "if it be Thy will" to our prayers is often a mere subterfuge of unbelief. True submission to God is not inconsistent with virility and boldness. Notice what Shammah did—simply *held his ground*. He was not seeking more worlds to conquer at that moment. He just stood where he was and hit out, right and left. Notice also the result of his action and to whom the glory is ascribed.

6. *Praying through to victory*. I repeat that this does not necessarily apply to every kind of prayer. A young Lisu Christian here is fond of telling an experience of his a few months ago. He was walking the fields in the evening when his insides began unaccountably to pain him. He dropped on his knees and, bowing his head down to the ground, asked Jesus to cure him. At once the stomachache left him. Praise the Lord! And there are no doubt multitudes of such cases—simple faith and simple answers.

But we must not rest content with such prayer. We must get beyond stomachache or any other ache and enter into the deeper fellowship of God's purposes. "That we henceforth be no more children" (Eph. 4:14). We must press on to maturity. We must attain to "the measure of the stature of the fullness of Christ," and not remain in God's kindergarten indefinitely. If we grow into manhood in the spiritual life we shall not escape conflict. As long as Ephesians 6:10-18 remains in the Bible, we must be prepared for serious warfare—"and having done all, to stand." We must fight through and then stand victorious on the battlefield.

Is not this another secret of many unanswered prayers—that they are not fought through? If the result is not seen as soon as expected, Christians are apt to lose heart and, if it is still longer delayed, to abandon it altogether.

We must count the cost before praying the prayer of faith. We must be willing to pay the price. We must mean business. We must set ourselves to "see things through" (Eph. 6:18, "with all perseverance"). Our natural strength will fail: and herein lies the necessity of a divinely given faith. We can then rest back in the everlasting Arms and renew our strength continually. We can then rest as well as wrestle. In this conflict-prayer, after the definite exercise of faith, there is no need to ask the thing again and again. It seems to me inconsistent to do so. Under these circumstances, I would say let the prayer take the following forms:

a. A firm standing on God-given ground, and a constant assertion of faith and claiming of victory. It is helpful, I find, to repeat passages of Scripture applicable to the subject. Let faith be continually strengthened and fed from its proper source, the Word of God.

b. A definite fighting and *resisting of Satan's host* in the name of Christ. As direct weapons against Satan, I like to read in prayer such passages as I John 3:8: "For this purpose the Son of God was manifested, that he might destroy the works of the devil," and Revelation 12:11: "They overcame him by the blood of the Lamb." I often find it a means of much added strength and liberty to fight in this way. Nothing cuts like the Word of the living God (Heb. 4:12).

c. Praying through every aspect of the matter in detail. In the case of my Lisu work here, I continually pray to God for a fresh knowledge of His will, more wisdom in dealing with the people, knowledge of how to pray, how to maintain the victory, how to instruct the people in the Gospel or in singing or in prayer, help in studying the language, help in ordinary conversation, help in preaching, guidance about choice of a central place to live in, guidance about building a house (if necessary), guidance in my personal affairs (money, food, clothes, etc.), help and blessing in my correspondence, openings for the Word and blessing in other villages, for leaders and helpers to be raised up for me, for each of the Christians by name, also for every one of my prayer helpers by name. Such detailed prayer is exhausting, but I believe effectual in ascertaining the will of God and obtaining His highest blessing.

I would not ask anyone to join me in the definite prayer for the turning to God of several hundred Lisu families unless God gives him individual guidance to do so. Better offer prayer in a more general way than make a definite petition apart from His leading. I should, however, value highly the prayer cooperation of any who feel led to join me in it. What I want, too, is not just an occasional mention of my work and its needs before the Lord, during the morning or evening devotions, but a definite time (say half an hour or so?) set apart for the purpose every day, either during the daytime or in the evening. Can you give that time to me—or rather, to the Lord?

About a fortnight ago I baptized two Lisu women at the little village of Six Family Hollow, the wives of two young Lisu men I baptized last January. I have now baptized six Christian Lisu altogether, all from that one family. It was my painful duty, however, only the next day, to exclude Ah-do from church fellowship. It appears that he has been continually breaking the seventh commandment, not only in his own villages but also in other places where he has been with me. The Lisu are a very immoral race in any case, but in spite of his Christian profession he has been even more promiscuous than most of them. He seems quite penitent and never attempted to deny his guilt. We must pray for his restoration.

I have no other special news of the work just now. I am thinking of visiting Six Family Hollow again in a few days, as well as other villages.

Hoping to write again next month, and with earnest prayers for you all,

YOURS IN THE LORD'S SERVICE,

J.O. FRASER

Here we find a missionary urgently requesting others to join with him in the practice of prayer. His readers were well aware of the millions of lost souls in China. They did not need to be reminded that the Scriptures abound with examples and commands to pray. J. O. Fraser outlined the biblical method of prayer because he felt that knowing better how to pray would encourage Christians to live up to their responsibility.

J. O. Fraser's effectiveness as a missionary is believed by many to stem from his personal prayer life and from the small prayer groups he encouraged in England.

During the years of Fraser's service among the Lisu people and in the years that followed, tens of thousands of these people came to know Christ. This ministry was multiplied in a marvelous way when some 30,000 Lisu migrated to Burma, where they linked up with Christian churches already established there. The 45,000 Lisu who remained in Southwest China continued to bear witness to Christ in the troubled years that followed.

Now, as then, the world is in desperate need of men and women like J. O. Fraser who will aggressively cooperate with God in His great plan of redemption. Our effectiveness in God's work will depend on how closely we walk with Him in prayer.

At the outset of this book, you were asked to consider the state of the practice of prayer in your life. Both heaven and earth are waiting to hear your answer. Will you commit yourself to pray? To keep on praying? To pray with passion?

QUESTIONS FOR REFLECTION AND PRAYER

1. Do you believe God has called or is calling you to a ministry of persevering prayer, whether with a general of definite focus? Have you accepted His call? Are you being faithful, or are you sometimes doing the work and sometimes not, or have you turned your back on the call entirely? Talk this over with the Lord now.

2. How has the Devil sought to discourage or impede your practice of prayer? How have you responded to his opposition? Have you called out to God for His help, or have you tried to win the battle on your own? Pray about this right now.

3. Do you find it difficult to persevere in prayer for a specific

request or burden, no matter how long it might take or what barriers get in the way? Why or why not? How can prayer be both a rest and a wrestling? What can you do to allow God to sustain you in your ministry of prayer? Discuss this with God now.

SCRIPTURE
INDEX

4:15	186
7:25	11
11	51, 178
11:1	48, 49
11:1-2	48
11:2	50
11:6	47
12:5-11	201
12:11	150

James

1:2	147, 148
1:2-4	104
1:5	152
1:6	152
3:3	165
3:4	165
3:5	165, 166
3:6	166
3:7-8	167
3:8	163, 167
3:9	167
3:10	167
3:11-12	167
4:3	99, 208
4:7	194, 212
4:7-8	10
4:17	124
5:16	99

1 Peter

3:7	97, 101
5:8	185
5:8-9	193

1 John

1:8, 10	199
1:8—2:2	199
1:9	18, 88, 106, 203
2:19	178
3:6-9	177, 200
3:8	213
4:4	103
4:13	78, 180
5:4	47
5:14	71
5:14-15	72, 78, 203, 208
5:16	201, 202

Revelation

3:20	180
12:10	98
12:11	106, 171, 213
21:27	128

GENERAL

INDEX